THE
DIGITAL TWIN 2.0

www.royalcollins.com

THE
DIGITAL
TWIN 2.0

The Future of Technology and Business

KEVIN CHEN

Books Beyond Boundaries

ROYAL COLLINS

The Digital Twin 2.0: The Future of Technology and Business

Second Edition

Published by Royal Collins Publishing Group Inc.
550-555 Boulevard René-Lévesque O,
Montréal, Québec, H2Z 1B1, Canada
www.royalcollins.com

ISBN: 978-1-4878-1182-2

First Edition Published in 2021
Second Edition Published in 2024

Cover and book design by the Royal Collins Publishing Group Design Team

10 9 8 7 6 5 4 3 2 1

CONTENTS

Introduction ix

Preface xi

CHAPTER 1

Overview 1

1.1   The Definition of "Digital Twin" 2

1.2   Digital Twins and Digital Threads 5

1.3   The Evolution of Digital Twin Technology 7

1.4   The Value and Significance of Digital Twin Technology 14

1.5   The Significance of Digital Twins for the Development of Metaverse 22

CHAPTER 2

Digital twin technology 27

2.1   Fields Related to Digital Twin 27

2.2   The Digital Twin Technological System 41

2.3   The Core Technology of Digital Twins 48

2.4   Creating Digital Twins 53

2.5   The Nine Key Elements That Determine Digital Twin 58

CHAPTER 3

Digital Twin and Industry 4.0 61

3.1   The Product Digital Twin 62
3.2   Digital Twin and PLM 70
3.3   The Interpretation of Digital Twin by Large Software Companies 80
3.4   Development Trends in Digital Twin Manufacturing 85

CHAPTER 4

Digital Twin City 89

4.1   The Rise of the Digital Twin City Concept 90
4.2   The Four Characteristics of Digital Twin City 93
4.3   Digital Twin City Service Form(s) and Typical Scenario(s) 94

CHAPTER 5

Other Digital Twin Applications 101

5.1   Healthcare 101
5.2   Smart Homes 102
5.3   Aerospace 104
5.4   Oil and Gas Exploration 104
5.5   Smart Logistics 104
5.6   Promoting Real World Search 107
5.7   Monitoring and Managing Brain Activity 108

CHAPTER 6

Digital Twin Applications 109

6.1   Aircraft Engine PLM Based on Digital Twin 109
6.2   Assembly of Complex Products Based on Digital Twin 115
6.3   APEX, BP's Advanced Simulation and Surveillance System 124
6.4   Comprehensive Enterprise Budgeting Systems Based on Digital Twin 126
6.5   Construction and Application of China's First In-Service Oil and Gas
      Pipeline Digital Twin 127

CHAPTER 7

The Challenges and Development Trends of Digital twin technology......................141

7.1 New Trends in the Development of Digital Twin Technology 141
7.2 The Five-Dimensional Model of Digital Twin 146
7.3 Fifteen Application Areas of the Digital Twin Five-Dimensional
Model...153

CHAPTER 8

Digital Economy Industrial Policy 185

8.1 Defining the Digital Economy 185
8.2 Digital Economy Strategies and Industrial Policies of Major Countries
and Regions around the World 186
8.3 An Analysis of the Key Points in Digital Economy Industry Support
Policies of Various Regions in China 198
8.4 Conclusion...217

Afterword 219
Notes 221
References..223
Index 225

INTRODUCTION

This book covers many important technical points related to digital twin technology and puts forward a number of innovative views. The content includes an overview of the digital twin concept, the underlying technology, its connection to Industry 4.0, digital twin city and other applications, the challenges and development trends for this technology, and digital economy industrial policies. By reading this book, the reader can obtain a deep understanding of the emerging discipline of digital twin. This book can help product design professionals and manufacturing companies determine future R&D goals and provide industries related to the digital economy with direction for their development, structural upgrade, and systematic improvement in order to increase innovative capabilities and competitiveness. It can also provide help and guidance to those in industries related to digital twin to deepen their understanding of the industry and enhance their professional knowledge and skills. Real-life examples have been included to help readers understand the subject matter, so this book can also serve as a textbook or reference book for teachers and students in the product design, industrial design, design management, and design marketing disciplines in tertiary institutions.

PREFACE

The digital economy is a new economic form, resulting from the IT revolution. It has become the main driver of economic growth, transforming and upgrading the preceding agricultural and industrial economies. It is also the strategic high ground in the latest round of global industrial competition.

On April 18, 2019, the Digital Economy Development and Employment in China white paper released by the China Academy of Information and Communications Technology revealed that the size of the country's digital economy reached RMB 31.3 trillion in 2018, a year-on-year increase of 20.9% and a 34.8% share of its GDP. Industrial digitalization has become the main engine of growth for the digital economy. In recent years, the growth rate and volume of the digital economy have attracted much attention. The reason is that the digital economy is developing significantly faster than traditional economic sectors, providing significant growth momentum.

Concentrating on developing the digital economy has become an important starting point for China to utilize Big Data and promote high-quality economic development. The digital economy has played a leading role in stabilizing growth and promoting structural adjustments and transformation. At present, China's overall digital economy framework is basically in place, and the specific policy system will quickly take shape. As part of this, the Internet Plus high-quality development policy system is about to be rolled out. This system includes policies to promote the overall development of the digital economy, regulatory or governance policies, related environmental policies, and policies related to the development of important digital economy industries such as Big Data, AI, and cloud computing. A series of major projects related to Internet Plus and the digital economy may follow.

As the development of the digital economy intensifies, new technologies such as the Internet, Big Data, and AI will become more deeply embedded in everyday life. As people spend an increasing amount of time on online social networks, online games, e-commerce, and working remotely, their digital identities become more prominent in society. It is conceivable that if humans spend more than 50% of their daily waking hours in the digital world, then humans' digital identities will be more real and effective than their identities in the physical world.

In February 2019, at the HIMSS Global Health Conference—one of the most influential, large-scale exhibitions in the worldwide health IT industry—AI-driven digital twin technology developed by Siemens AG was unveiled. The company's aim was to use digital technology to understand a patient's health and predict the efficacy of treatment plans. The digital twin of science fiction is fast becoming a reality. So what exactly is this mythical sounding "digital twin"? What kind of functions does it have? What kind of benefits can it bring to companies? How is it created? In which sectors has it currently found practical application? It can be said that digital twin technology will become a cornerstone of industrial activities in the future. It is a disruptive technology for product lifecycle management that will bring revolutionary changes to the manufacturing, construction, and aerospace industries. There is no doubt that the digital twin revolution will create new production factors for modern industry.

This book provides innovative ideas about the digital economy and digital twin technology in the context of the 5G revolution, supply-side reform, and Internet Plus. It gives a close-up view of the areas of interest, difficulties, and priorities for digital twin technology R&D in the context of developing the digital economy. The content includes an overview of the digital twin concept, the underlying technology, its connection to Industry 4.0, digital twin city and other applications, the challenges and development trends for this technology, and digital economy industrial policies. It is an exposition of digital twin knowledge and the professional skills required. At the same time, a lot of figures and examples closely related to theory have been incorporated throughout this book to make it more vivid, interesting, comprehensible, and easier to digest for readers.

This book is edited by Chen Gen. The editor would like to express his deep gratitude to Chen Daoshuang, Chen Daoli, Chen Xiaoqin, Chen Yinkai, Lu Dejian, Gao Aqin, Xiang Yuhua, Li Zihui, Zhu Yuding, Zhou Meili, Li Wenhua, Lin Yihui, Huang Lianhuan, and others, for the tremendous help they gave in the preparation of this book.

Due to time constraints and knowledge gaps, some research outcomes with practical reference value were cited in this book. They include: "The Five-dimensional Digital Twin Model and 10 Major Applications," published in the January 2019 issue of *Computer Integrated Manufacturing Systems* by Professor Tao Fei, et al.; "Building and Using an In-service Oil and Gas Pipeline Digital Twin for the First Time in China," published in the February 2019 issue of *Oil and Gas Storage and Transportation* by Mr. Xiong Ming, et al.; and "The Connotation, Architecture and Development Trend of Product Digital Twins," published in the April 2017 issue of *Computer Integrated Manufacturing Systems* by Mr. Zhuang Cunbo and his fellow researchers. The editor would like to take the chance to express his sincere thanks to them.

KEVIN CHEN

CHAPTER 1

OVERVIEW

New technologies such as the Internet, Big Data, and artificial intelligence (AI) are becoming a larger part of our daily lives. As we spend more time on social networks, online games, e-commerce, and working remotely, our digital identities become more prominent in society. It is conceivable that if humans spend more than 50% of their daily waking hours in the digital world, then humans' digital identities will be more real and effective than their identities in the physical world. In the past few years, a new term has become popular in the field of Internet of Things (IoT): digital twin.

From 2017 to 2019, the digital twin was selected as one of the top ten strategic technology trends by Gartner for three consecutive years. Strategic technology trends mean trends with significant disruptive potential that are developing and growing from an emerging state, with the potential to have a broader impact and application scope or are rapidly growing with great volatility. In February 2019, at the annual global meeting of the Healthcare Information and Management Systems Society (HIMSS)—one of the most influential events in the worldwide healthcare IT sector—artificial intelligence medical treatment was a topic that many participants were interested in. Of particular interest was an AI-driven digital twin technology that Siemens was developing, aiming to use digital technology to understand the health of patients and predict the effectiveness of treatment options.

On March 10, 2019, the crash of Ethiopian Airlines Flight 302 resulted in the regrettable loss of many lives. It is painful to think about it. Two major accidents in less than half a year, both involving Boeing 737 MAX 8 airliners, triggered discussions about the daily maintenance of aircraft. This even led to a trading halt for shares of companies that are pioneers in the field of digital twin as their prices rocketed. Digital twin technology is receiving greater attention.

In 2020, according to Deloitte's latest technology trend report, the digital twin has become the most important technology trend for cognition and analysis. The report cited research data from MarketsandMarkets and IDC, showing that the exploration of digital twin technology has already begun: the value of digital twin market was $3.8 billion in 2019 and is expected to increase to $35.8 billion by 2025.

Let us take a moment to imagine the future. Astronauts on a space mission need to perform an urgent extravehicular repair job in distant outer space. They have neither time nor space to rehearse and no prior experience to rely on. Given the extremely dangerous conditions and just one chance to get it done, what are their options?

Instead of panicking, our astronauts use various operational parameters like the external environment, time, temperature, etc., to simulate a virtual environment that replicates reality. Through repeated experiments in virtual reality (VR), the best operational method and process is derived. This is then used to program the space robot that is going to perform the task, minimizing the dangers and mistakes.

These are not distant and unlikely scenarios. In science fiction films, digital twins are quickly becoming the reality. What exactly is this mythical-sounding "digital twin"? What kind of functions can it achieve? What benefits can it bring to business? How is a digital twin created? What role(s) does it currently play and in which areas?

1.1   The Definition of "Digital Twin"

1.1.1   A general definition of "digital twin"

In layman's terms, digital twin refers to using digital means, such as various wearable devices, including wearable industrial devices and human wearable devices, to construct an entity identical to the physical object in the digital world. This allows for a better understanding, analysis, and optimization of the physical entity and enables real-time interconnection and interaction between the virtual and real world. From a more professional perspective, a digital twin: integrates AI, machine learning (ML), and other technologies; combines data, algorithms, and decision analysis to build simulations (i.e., the virtual mapping of physical objects); forecasts problems; monitors changes in the virtual models of physical objects; diagnoses complex processing and abnormal analysis of multidimensional data based on AI; and predicts potential risks before making reasonable, effective plans or maintaining the relevant equipment.

A digital twin is the process and method of forming a model of a production process in the physical world and its digital mirror image in the digital world (Figure 1-1).[6] From the figure, we can see its five major elements: sensors, data, integration, analysis, and actuators, as well as constantly updated digital twin applications.

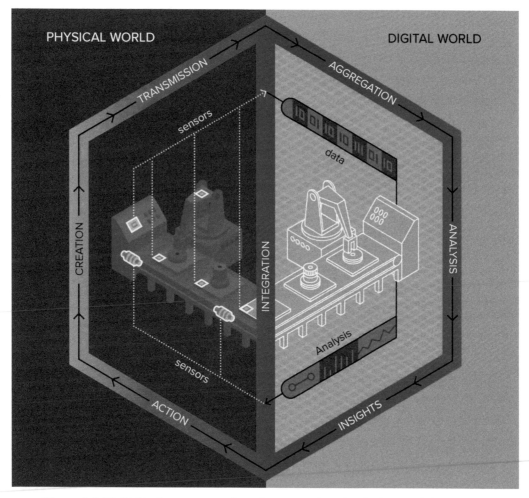

Figure 1-1 Digital twins are mappings between the physical and digital worlds

1) Sensors. Sensors in the production process are configured to send out signals, and the digital twin can obtain operational and environmental data from actual processes through these signals.

2) Data. The actual operational and environmental data provided by the sensors will be merged with enterprise data after aggregation. Enterprise data includes bills of materials, enterprise systems, and design specifications. Other types of data include engineering drawings, external data sources, and customer complaint records.

3) Integration. Sensors enable data transmission between the physical world and the digital world through integrated technologies (including boundaries, communication interfaces, and security).

4) Analysis. The digital twin uses analytical techniques to carry out algorithmic simulations and visualization procedures to analyze data, provide insights, and establish quasi-real-time digital models of physical entities and processes. The digital twin identifies deviations from an ideal state at different levels.

5) Actuators. If it is determined that action should be taken, the digital twin will take actual action with human intervention through actuator(s) with manual intervention.

In practice, processes (or physical entities) and their digital virtual images are significantly more complex than simple models or structures.

1.1.2   Definition by the Industry 4.0 terms writing group

The Industry 4.0 terms writing group defined "digital twin" as a digital data stream built with advanced modeling and simulation tools, covering the entire product lifecycle and value chain, and integrating basic materials, design, process, manufacturing, use, and maintenance. This data stream is integrated into a unified model and drives product design, manufacturing, and security.

Analyzing these concepts reveals that the digital link provides the digital twin with access, as well as integration and conversion capabilities. The aim is to achieve full traceability, two-way sharing/interactive information, and value chain collaboration for the entire product lifecycle and value chain.[7]

Figure 1-2 below depicts a digital twin conceptual framework by the renowned intelligent manufacturing expert, Professor Zhang Shu.[8] Through it, we can derive a more intuitive understanding of the definition by the Industry 4.0 terms writing group.

Fundamentally speaking, a digital twin is a dynamic representation of the past and present behavior or process(es) of a physical entity through digitization, which helps to improve corporate performance.

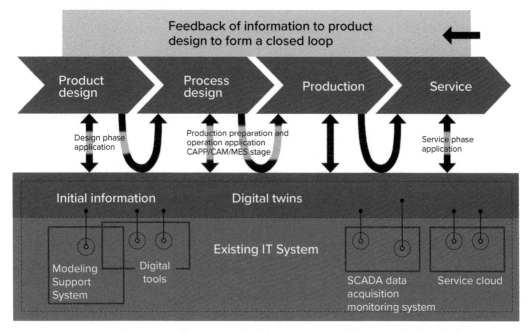

Figure 1-2 Digital twin conceptual framework by Professor Zhang Shu

1.2   Digital Twins and Digital Threads

With the development of the digital twin concept, the US Air Force Research Laboratory (AFRL) and the National Aeronautics and Space Administration (NASA) jointly proposed the "digital thread" concept.

Digital threads are scalable and configurable enterprise-level analysis frameworks that inform decision makers throughout the system's lifecycle by providing access, integration, and the ability to transform different or decentralized data into actionable information. It also allows for dynamic, real-time evaluation of products in the capability planning and analysis, preliminary design, detailed design, manufacturing, testing and maintenance acquisition phases, facilitating decision-making now and in the future. Digital threads are also communication frameworks that allow for connectable data streams and provide integrated views of isolated functions at all stages of system lifecycles. A digital thread provides the conditions for delivering the right information to the right place at the right time, so that models at all links in a system's full lifecycle can perform two-way synchronization and communication of key data in real time.

By analyzing and comparing the definitions of digital twin and digital thread, one can see that while digital twins deal with objects, models, and data, digital threads are concerned with methods, channels, links, and interfaces. Information about digital twins is ex-changed and processed through digital threads. Taking the product design and manufacturing process as an example, the relationship between its digital twins and digital threads is shown in Figure 1-3.

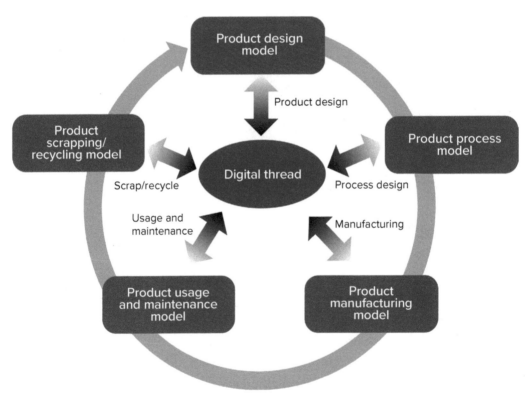

Figure 1-3 The relationship between the digital twins and digital threads of a product

Figure 1-4 shows an application that combines a product's digital twin(s) and digital thread(s).[9] The parameters of the simulation analysis model can be transferred to the full three-dimensional model of the product definition and then to the digital production line for processing or assembly into a physical product which is then reflected into the product definition model using online digital inspection or measurement system(s). Finally, feedback is then provided to the simulation analysis model.

Through the digital thread, the two-way interaction of the model(s) and key data of each stage of the entire product lifecycle is realized, so that the models are kept consistent. Finally, the closed-loop management of product lifecycle data and models is achieved.

Simply put, the digital thread runs through the entire product lifecycle, especially the seamless integration of product design, production, operation, and maintenance. As for the product's digital twin, it is more like the mapping of smart products, which emphasizes feedback in areas from product operation and maintenance to product design.

Product digital twins are digital images of physical products. Through integration with external sensors, all the characteristics (both macro and micro) of objects are captured, showing the product's evolution during its lifecycle. Other than the product, digital twins should also be built for production (production lines and equipment) and maintenance systems as needed.[10]

1.3   The Evolution of Digital Twin Technology

1.3.1   NASA's Apollo program

The earliest usage of the digital twin concept can be traced back to NASA's Project Apollo.

For the project, NASA had two identical spacecraft manufactured. The spacecraft which remained on Earth was referred to as the "twin" and was used to mirror the status of the spacecraft performing the mission. During flight preparation, the twin was used extensively for training. During mission execution, the twin was used for simulated experiments in conditions that replicate the environment of space. As far as possible, the status of the spacecraft carrying out the mission in space was accurately reflected and forecasted in order to assist the astronauts in orbit in making the best decision in emergencies.

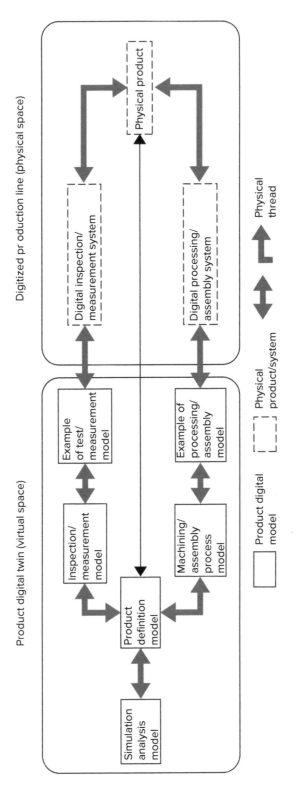

Figure 1-4 An example of an application that combines a product's digital twins with digital threads

This shows that the twin is a prototype or model that mirrors the actual operation of the object in real time through simulation. It has two notable features:

1) The twin is identical to the object it mirrors in terms of appearance (referring to the geometric shape and size of the product), content (referring to the structural composition of the product and both its macroscopic and microscopic physical characteristics), and properties (referring to the function and performance of the product).

2) It is allowed to mirror the actual operating status or conditions of the object through simulation and other methods. It should be pointed out that the "twin" referred to here is still a physical entity.

1.3.2 Dr. Michael Grieves proposes the digital twin concept

In 2003, Dr. Michael Grieves introduced the concept of "the equivalent virtual digital expression of physical products" in his product lifecycle management(PLM) course at the University of Michigan. According to him, a digital copy of a specific device or set of devices is an abstract representation of the actual device(s) and can be used as a basis for testing under real or simulated conditions. The concept stems from the desire to express information and data about the device(s) more clearly, hoping to put all the information together for a higher level of analysis. Although the concept was not named "digital twin" at that time (from 2003 to 2005, it was referred to as the "Mirrored Spaced Model" and from 2006 to 2010 as the "Information Mirroring Model"), it contained all the components of the digital twin concept, namely physical space, virtual space and the relationship or interface between the two, so it can be considered the prototype of the digital twin concept. In 2011, Dr. Grieves cited the term "digital twin," which his collaborator John Vickers used to describe the conceptual model in his book *Virtually Perfect: Driving Innovative and Lean Products through Product Lifecycle Management,* and the term has been to refer to the concept ever since.

The conceptual model (Figure 1-5) includes physical products in physical space, virtual products in virtual space, and data and information interaction interfaces between physical and virtual space.

The digital twin conceptual model described by Vickers greatly expanded the concept of the "twin" of the NASA Apollo program (Table 1-1).

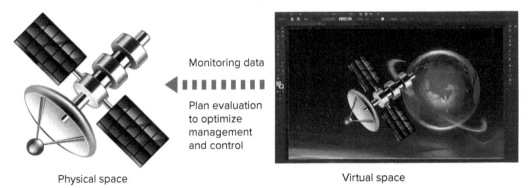

Monitoring data

Plan evaluation
to optimize
management
and control

Physical space

Virtual space

Figure 1-5 The digital twin conceptual model

Table 1-1 The digital twin concept builds on the concept of "twin" from the NASA Apollo program

1	Digitization of the "twin" and using digital expressions to create a virtual product that is the same in appearance, content, and nature as the product entity.
2	Introduce virtual space, establish the association between virtual space and physical space, and exchange data and information between the two.
3	Graphical and intuitive representation of the fusion of virtual and real, and using the virtual to control the real.
4	Expand and extend the "twin" concept. In addition to products, corresponding digital twins are established for factories, production lines, and manufacturing resources (work stations, equipment, personnel and materials, etc.).

Limited by the scientific and technological conditions at that time, the conceptual model did not attract the attention of scholars either domestically or abroad when it was proposed in 2003. However, as technology advanced and scientific research conditions improved, the digital twin concept has come to be applied in the fields of analog simulation, virtual assembly, and 3D printing.

1.3.3 The United States AFRL used digital twins to resolve the problem of maintaining fighter plane airframes

When the US AFRL formulated its long-term vision for the next 30 years back in 2011, it incorporated the digital twin concept, hoping in the future to have every fighter plane delivered with its digital twin. It also proposed the "airframe digital twin" concept in which such digital twins serve as hyper-realistic models of airframes being manufactured and maintained and can be used to simulate and evaluate whether the airframes satisfy mission requirements, as shown in Figure 1-6.

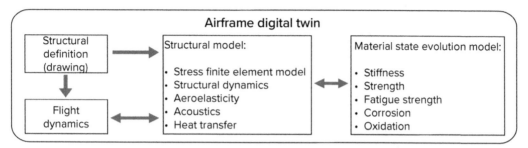

Figure 1-6 The AFRL proposed using the digital twin concept to tackle the issue of maintaining fighter plane airframes

An airframe digital twin refers to the standardized model(s) and computing model(s) in the product lifecycle of an aircraft. It is related to the materials, manufacturing specifications, and processes used to manufacture and maintain the aircraft. It is also a sub model of the aircraft digital twin. An aircraft digital twin is an integrated model that contains the electronic system model, flight control system model, propulsion system model, and other subsystem models. At this time, the aircraft digital twin has progressed from the conceptual model stage to the preliminary planning and implementation stage, with more in-depth descriptions of what it entails, as reflected in the five aspects shown in Table 1-2.

Table 1-2 The aircraft digital twin has progressed from the conceptual model stage to the preliminary planning and implementation stage

1	It highlights the hierarchy and integratedness of digital twins, such as aircraft digital twins, airframe digital twins, airframe structural models, material state evolution models, etc., which facilitate the gradual implementation and final realization of digital twins.
2	It highlights the hyperrealism of digital twins, including geometric models, physical models, and material state evolution models.
3	It highlights the extensive nature of digital twins, which includes the entire product lifecycle and extends from design to the subsequent manufacturing and product service stages.

(Continued)

| 4 | It highlights the consistency of digital twins throughout the product lifecycle and reflects the idea of a single data source. |
| 5 | The computability of digital twins is highlighted, and the real state of the corresponding product entities can be mirrored in real time through simulation and analysis. |

1.3.4   Cooperation between NASA and AFRL

In 2010, NASA began exploring Condition Based Monitoring. In 2012, NASA and AFRL worked together to jointly propose the digital twin concept for future vehicles, in light of requirements for lighter aircrafts with longer lifespans, operating longer in more extreme environments, and bearing heavier loads. For aircraft, flight systems, or launch vehicles, digital twins were defined as a multiphysics, multiscale, probabilistic simulation model for aircraft or system integration, which utilizes the best physical models available, updated sensor data, and historical data to reflect the status of the flying entity corresponding to the model.

In the Modeling, Simulation, Information Technology and Processing Roadmap published by both organizations in 2012, digital twin was listed as a technical challenge to implementing simulation-based system engineering during the period 2023–2028. Since then, the digital twin concept has been brought into the public domain. This definition can be regarded as a summary by NASA and the AFRL of their research outcomes thus far, highlighting the integratedness and multiphysics, multiscale, and probabilistic nature of digital twins whose main function is to reflect real-time status of the flying entity it is tagged to (a continuation of the function of the "twin" from the early years of the Apollo program). The data used includes the best physical model(s) of the products available at that time, updated sensor data and historical data of the product lineup.

1.3.5   The advanced nature of digital twin technology has been absorbed by many industries

In 2012, General Electric (GE) used digital means to realize Assets Performance Management (APM). In 2014, as the IoT, AI, and virtual reality continued to develop, more industrial products and equipment came with smart characteristics, and the digital twin concept gradually expanded to encompass the entire product lifecycle, including production and services. At the same time, the form and concept of the digital twin continue to be enriched. However, the high levels of integration necessary and the interdisciplinary nature of the concept mean it is difficult to achieve sufficient technical maturity within a short period, so progressive research on its substance and application is particularly important. A classic example is the F-15 fighter plane airframe jointly built by NASA and AFRL to assess the health and predict damage to the airframes of planes that are in service to provide early warning, and guidance on repair and replacement. In addition, GE plans to use digital twins to implement real-time monitoring and predictive maintenance of engines. Dassault Aviation plans to use its 3Dexperience platform to interact with the digital twins of its products and has successfully demonstrated the concept with aircraft radars.

Although the digital twin concept originated in aerospace, its advanced nature means that other industries are turning to it. Research based on Building Information Modeling (BIM) has led to digital twin(s) for the construction industry; BIM, digital twins, augmented reality, and the maintenance of nuclear power facilities are now discussed jointly; medical researchers have even used digital twin concept to build "virtual fetuses" for the screening of genetic diseases.

As early as 2017, Gartner included digital twin technology among the top ten strategic technology trends of the year, pointing to its huge potential as a disrupter. In the next three to five years, hundreds of millions of physical entities with have digital twins.

In China, under the strategic backdrop of Internet Plus and the drive for the country to become a manufacturing powerhouse, the potential of digital twin technology in smart manufacturing has also caught the attention of many scholars. They have discussed the background, conceptual connotation, framework, implementation approaches, and development trends of the digital twin, as well as its application in configuration management, and they have proposed the Digital Twin Workshop concept. They have also embarked on theoretical and practical studies to see how the physical and information aspects of the manufacturing industry can be integrated and interact with each other.

In the process of maturing and perfecting the concept of digital twins, the application of digital twins is no longer limited to using the IoT to observe and improve the operational performance of products. Still it has extended to broader fields, such as digital twins of factories, digital twins of cities, and even digital twins of Earth.

Overall, digital twins establish a communication bridge between the real world and the virtual world across different levels and scales and are an effective means of achieving the interaction and integration of the manufacturing information world and the physical world. Therefore, digital twins are also regarded as one of the universal purpose technologies and core technology systems of the Fourth Industrial Revolution, supporting the comprehensive technology system of the IoT and serving as the information infrastructure of the future intelligent era.

The essence of the metaverse is the construction of a digital twin of Earth, including the artificial intelligence revolution represented by ChatGPT. The underlying core of this is also based on the digital twin of Earth to construct an Earth intelligent management mode.

1.4 The Value and Significance of Digital Twin Technology

1.4.1 The value of digital twin technology

What can digital twin do for businesses?

An unavoidable and important question in the development of technology is whether it can create actual value for enterprises. In the past, the cost of creating digital twins was high and the benefit meager. However, as storage and computing costs fall, the applications for and potential benefits of digital twins have risen sharply, making them more commercially viable.

When exploring the business value of digital twins, companies must focus on issues related to strategic performance and market dynamics, including the continuous improvement of product performance, accelerating the design cycle, exploring potential sources of revenue, and optimizing warranty cost management. Based on these strategic issues, the corresponding applications can be developed, thereby leveraging on digital twin technology to create business value in many areas. The various business values of digital twin technology are shown in Table 1-3.

Table 1-3　The business value of digital twin technology[11]

Type of business value	Potential business value
Quality	• Improve overall quality • Anticipate and quickly discover quality defect trends • Control quality vulnerabilities and determine when quality issues will occur

(Continued)

Type of business value	Potential business value
Warranty costs and services	• Understand current equipment configuration and optimize service efficiency • Identify warranty and claim issues to reduce overall warranty costs and improve customer experience
Operating costs	• Improve product design and effectively implement engineering changes • Improve production equipment performance • Reduce operational and process changes
Record keeping and serialization	• Create digital files to record parts and raw material serial numbers, so as to more effectively manage recalled products and warranty applications, and perform mandatory tracking
Cost of introducing new product and delivery cycle	• Shorten time to market for new products • Reduce the overall production cost of new products • Effectively identify components with long lead times and their impact on the supply chain
Income growth opportunities	• Identify products to be upgraded • Improve efficiency, reduce costs, and optimize products

In addition to those business values, manufacturers can also use digital twins to establish key performance indicators. To summarize, digital twins can be used in many applications to enhance business value and promote fundamental business transformation. The value generated can be measured by tangible results, that, in turn, can be traced back to a company's key indicators.

Today, major manufacturers are increasingly focusing on digital twin technology and using it as a solution and means of serving enterprises. These illustrate its huge potential.

1) Simulate, monitor, diagnose, predict, and control the formation process and behavior of products in a real environment.

   As shown in Figure 1-7, factories can establish assembly simulations for engineers to better understand product structure and operating status.
2) Fundamentally promote efficient collaboration throughout the product lifecycle and drive continuous innovation (Figure 1-8).

Figure 1-7 Assembly simulation allows engineers to better understand product structure and operating status

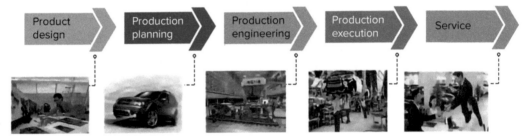

Figure 1-8 Fundamentally promote efficient collaboration throughout the product lifecycle and drive continuous innovation

Figure 1-9 Using digital twins to simulate digital models to derive optimal solutions

As a leader in the field of simulation, Ansys works closely with GE to integrate its simulation software with GE's industrial data and Predix analysis cloud platform. This combination of simulation capabilities and data analysis functions can help companies gain strategic insights.

GE produces a digital twin for every engine, turbine, and nuclear magnetic resonance device. By debugging and testing in virtual reality using a realistic digital model, GE finds out how to maximize machine efficiency before optimizing the scheme to be applied to the actual model (Figure 1-9).

3) The digital product full lifecycle file lays a data foundation for whole process traceability and continuous improvement to research and development (Figure 1-10).

4) Many ways of creating value. With digital twins, any manufacturer can create, generate, test, and verify in a data-driven virtual environment. This will become core competitiveness in the coming years.

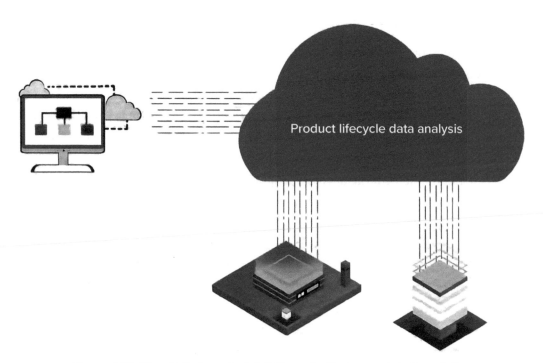

Figure 1-10 The digital product full lifecycle file lays a data foundation for whole process traceability and continuous improvement to research and development

1.4.2   The significance of digital twin technology

Since the digital twin concept was proposed, its technology has been evolving rapidly, and it has provided a huge boost for the design and manufacture of products, as well as how they serve.

Today's digital technology is constantly changing every enterprise. In the future, all enterprises will be digitized. This not only requires enterprises to develop products with digital characteristics but also refers to changing the entire product lifecycle through digital means and connecting a company's internal and external environments through digital means.

The shortening of product lifecycles, increased customization, and the need for companies to coordinate with both upstream and downstream partners have forced companies to adopt digital means to accelerate product development and improve both the effectiveness of production and services as well as the openness of its internal and external environments.

The digital twin concept is a far cry from the decades-old conventional design and manufacturing concepts that are based on experience. It enables designers to verify design concepts without developing physical prototypes, verify product reliability without complex physical experiments, predict production bottlenecks without conducting small-batch trial production, and even to gain insights into the operation of products sold without going to the site. Therefore, this digital transformation may be very difficult for traditional industrial players to undertake and adapt to, but it is indeed advanced and in line with the development of science and technology.

Undoubtedly, it will come to permeate the entire product lifecycle. Not only will it accelerate the product development process, it will improve the effectiveness and economy of development and production, provide a better understanding of product usage and help customers avoid losses, and even provide accurate usage feedback to the design team for effective product improvement.

All these require enterprises to have comprehensive digital capabilities based on digital twins. The practical significance of digital twin technology is mainly reflected in the four aspects shown in Table 1-4.

Table 1-4 The practical significance of digital twin technology

1	More convenient and suitable for innovation
2	More comprehensive measurements
3	More comprehensive analysis and prediction capabilities
4	Digitization of experience

1) More convenient and suitable for innovation. Through digitization means such as design tools, simulation tools, IoT, VR, etc., digital twin technology maps various attributes of physical devices into virtual space, forming digital images that can be dissembled and are reproducible, transferable, modifiable, deleteable, and reusable.

   This greatly speeds up the operator's understanding of the physical entity and allows many operations (such as simulation, batch copy, virtual assembly, etc.) that could otherwise not be completed due to physical constraints and the need for physical entities at one's fingertips, thereby inspiring people to explore new ways to optimize design, manufacturing, and services.

2) More comprehensive measurements. "Anything that can be measured can be improved" is an unchanging truth in industry. Whether it is design, manufacturing, or services, it is necessary to accurately measure various attributes, parameters, and the operating status of physical entities in order to achieve accurate analysis and optimization.

   However, traditional measurement methods rely on expensive physical tools such as sensors, acquisition systems, detection systems, etc., to obtain effective measurements. This naturally limits the scope of measurement. Many measurements that cannot be collected directly often have to be left out.

   Digital twins can use IoT and Big Data technology to collect direct data from limited physical sensor indicators and use large sample libraries to infer indicators that could not be directly measured through machine learning. For example, historical data on a series of indicators such as lubricating oil temperature, winding temperature, and rotor torque can be used to build different fault-characteristic models through machine learning to indirectly infer the health of a generator system.

19

3) More comprehensive analysis and prediction capabilities. Currently, PLM rarely produces accurate predictions, so it is often impossible to foresee obscure problems. By combining IoT data collection, Big Data processing, and AI modeling and analysis, digital twins are able to evaluate the current status, diagnose past issues, and provide the analytic results to simulate various possibilities so as to predict future trends, thereby providing more comprehensive support for decision-making.

4) Digitization of experience. In traditional industrial design, manufacturing, and service fields, experience is often something elusive and difficult to quantify or digitalize for accurate decision-making. In contrast, the digital twin is superior, and one of its key advancements is the digitization of expert experience that previously could not be saved into something that can be saved, copied, modified, and transferred.

For example, for the various fault features that occur during the operation of large equipment, historical data from sensors can be processed through machine learning to produce digitalized feature models for different types of fault phenomena. The models are then combined with records from experts to form a basis for making accurate judgments about future equipment faults. At the same time, the feature database can be updated and enriched with faults with new forms to ultimately produce autonomous intelligent diagnosis and judgment.

Therefore, before the arrival of the metaverse, one very core and crucial technology needed for the successful construction and development of the metaverse is digital twins. With digital twins, we can digitize and virtualize the physical world. Therefore, if we are interested in the metaverse and want to think about the trend of the metaverse industry, we should focus on digital twin technology. Simply put, if we don't have the concept of the metaverse today, based on the current industrial technology, that is, based on digital twin technology and the development of the wearable devices industry, when these two industries are combined and truly enter popular applications, the appearance of the metaverse is outlined. Because in the development of these two industrial technologies toward popularization and maturity, a series of problems behind them, such as chips, computing power, transmission, data security, and virtual reality interaction, will all be breakthroughs.

Instead of indulging in science fiction novels to construct the metaverse, it is better to understand digital twin technology calmly. We can start building the digital twin body of virtual reality from various levels, such as digital twin cities, digital twin manufacturing, digital twin healthcare, digital twin R&D, etc., based on the industrialization of digital twin technology. And based on digital twin technology, we can manage the physical world. In the future, digital twin technology will provide rich digital twin models for various virtual objects in the metaverse and associate virtual objects in the metaverse environment with their digital twin objects in the real world through real-time data collected from sensors and other connected devices, so that virtual objects in the metaverse environment can mirror, analyze, and predict the behavior of their digital twin objects. Therefore, as a dynamic simulation of the real world, the "digital twin" is one of the tentacles that the metaverse stretches out from the future.

1.4.3   A new production mode

Since the concept was proposed, digital twin technology has evolved rapidly and played a significant role in product design, manufacturing, and services.

Today's digital technology is constantly changing every enterprise. In the future, all enterprises will become digital companies, and our planet will also enter the era of the digital twin Earth. Some people have rebranded the digital twin earth concept as the metaverse. Whether the term "metaverse" exists, the digital twin earth is already on the road to exploration and development. For enterprises, this not only requires the development of products with digital features but also means changing the entire lifecycle process of the product through digital means and connecting the internal and external environment of the enterprise.

For example, in the field of e-commerce or online shopping, some have proposed a virtual fitting room concept, and some software or virtual fitting mirrors are available. However, these products cannot truly realize the idea of virtual and realistic fitting. The core reason is that digitizing clothes is easy, although there are still issues with digitizing clothes.

The bigger problem is that we, as physical entities, cannot be accurately digitized. So, both are uncertain when our physical bodies cannot be precisely digitized, and clothing cannot be precisely digitized. When these two uncertainties are combined, the virtual fitting becomes a fantasy, especially for clothing, requiring relatively high accuracy and fit. However, this problem can be solved in the era of digital twins. Digital twin humans and digital twin clothes can be used. The digital twin clothes can automatically adjust and generate data for the producer after trying on any ill-fitting sizes, achieving efficient personalized customization.

It is worth mentioning that although digital twins of humans have not yet emerged today, digital virtual humans already exist. Both share the commonality of being based on the digitization of humans, or in other words, the virtual digitization of humans.

However, the key difference is that a human's digital twin captures and synchronizes a person's real-time physical state. In contrast, a digital virtual human provides an approximate or abstract representation that does not accurately reflect the real-time physical state of a person. Therefore, with the concept of digital twin technology, it is easy and clear to anticipate the era of the metaverse or the realization of digital twins of humans, as we only need to look at the maturity of digital twin technology.

Therefore, in the context of Industry 4.0, the talk of flexible customization and personalized rapid manufacturing models is prevalent. The shortening of product lifecycles, the strengthening of product customization levels, and the necessity for enterprises to establish a collaborative ecological environment with upstream and downstream partners all force enterprises to adopt digital means to accelerate product development speed, improve the effectiveness of development, production, and services, and enhance the openness of internal and external environments. This manufacturing method, this production method, is the production method constructed by the era of digital twins.[12]

1.5   The Significance of Digital Twins for the Development of Metaverse

On November 2, 2021, Xinhua News Agency published an article stating that the metaverse is based on augmented reality technology to provide immersive experiences and utilizes digital twin technology to generate mirrors of the real world. As the metaverse connects the real and virtual worlds, it has been seen as the future of human digital existence. It can be said that digital twin technology is an essential part of the development process of the metaverse for it to reach its full potential.

1.5.1   The evolution of the metaverse requires digital twin technology

The metaverse creates a parallel and interconnected virtual world rooted in the real world. However, technology is the premise of the metaverse's emergence, and technology integration is the background of the metaverse's explosion. A metaverse is a new form of internet application and social structure that integrates various new technologies, such as continuous improvement of computing power, high-speed wireless communication networks, cloud computing, blockchain, virtual engines, VR/AR, digital twins, and other technological innovations that gradually converge. Generating a mirror image of the natural world based on digital twin technology is an indispensable part of the development of the metaverse. The virtual reality constructed by the metaverse blends with social forms, which, strictly speaking, is a mixed form of digital twin technology and real physical space, where we can freely travel between the real and virtual worlds.

Specifically, the metaverse connects the virtual and real worlds, enriches human perception, enhances experiences, extends creativity, and creates more possibilities. The virtual world transitions from simulating and replicating the physical world to extending and expanding it, which then impacts the physical world, ultimately blurring the boundaries between the virtual and real worlds. From this perspective, the rise of the metaverse can also be seen as the second attempt at transforming digital space towards three-dimensionality.

Although people cannot accurately depict the landscape of the metaverse, people are already living in the metaverse in various ways. People continuously construct the digital world, digitizing themselves and the physical world. The metaverse process changes are also influenced by different real-world variables, such as education, employment, consumption, and so on, affecting production and life of the real society.

For the metaverse, different stages have different levels of maturity. If informatization and digitization are the primary stages of the rise of the metaverse, then digital twin technology is the intermediate stage of the development of the metaverse. In 2011, Professor Michael Grieves cited his collaborator John Vickers' term "digital twin" to describe the concept model in Virtually Perfect: Driving Innovation and Lean through PLM. This term has been in use ever since. The digital twin is the "soul" of physical entities. After experiencing the technological preparation, concept generation, and application exploration period, digital twin technology is entering the leading application period, with the digital twinning of libraries, museums, and various scenic spots accelerating. The goal of developing digital twin technology is to move toward the metaverse.

1.5.2 From the development of digital twins to the metaverse

After being opened up for civilian use by NASA and the Department of Defense in the United States, the application of digital twin technology as the core of industrial technology has expanded from aerospace and defense industries to areas such as urban management. Whether it is for the industrial manufacturing industry, construction, urban operations and management, and management related to human health and physical characteristics, they will all be based on digital twin technology. It can be said that digital twins are an important technology in the modern industrial technology revolution, bringing us a major transformation of the means of production.

In April 2020, the National Development and Reform Commission and the Office of Central Cyberspace Administration of China issued the "Implementation Plan for Promoting the Action of 'Cloud Computing, Big Data, and AI Empower the Real Economy,'" proposing the launch of a digital twin innovation plan as a major measure to break through the key core technologies of digital transformation. In April 2020 and February 2021, relevant departments of the Ministry of Industry and Information Technology and the State Administration for Market Regulation issued two drafts of the "Guidelines for the Construction of Intelligent Ship Standard System (Solicitation of Comments)" for constructing the intelligent ship standard system, incorporating digital twins into the key technology application standard system. In September 2021, the Ministry of Industry and Information Technology and Housing and Urban-Rural Development issued the "Three-Year Action Plan for the Construction of New Infrastructure for the Internet of Things," pointing out the need to accelerate the research, development, and application of digital twin technology. It can be said that all industries, including battlefield training and war management in military wars, cannot do without the management system constructed by digital twin technology as the core. At the same time, digital twin technology is also a key underlying technology for successfully constructing the metaverse in the future. Compared with digital twins, the metaverse is a larger digital concept.

When we talk about the metaverse today, a large part of the people and the hype and emotions in the market come from some people in the previous digital currency speculation field. Some organizations currently established regarding the metaverse are more marketing-oriented with little substantive significance.

It can be said that when people worldwide talk about the metaverse and depict it, they are essentially like blind men touching an elephant. These statements cannot be said to be correct or incorrect, because all those who describe the appearance of the metaverse are just touching a part of the "elephant" based on their limited knowledge and then begin to imagine what the metaverse looks like in their cognition.

Why is talking about the metaverse currently like blind men touching an elephant? The core reason lies in the essence of the metaverse. Essentially, the metaverse is an interaction, a behavior based on the interconnection and intercommunication of virtual and physical reality worlds constructed based on multiple cutting-edge technologies.

It is difficult to describe what this interaction will be like today, as the technologies supporting the metaverse are not yet mature. Even VR, developed for many years, is still in the stage of application difficulties.

Although we cannot describe the future appearance of the metaverse clearly, we can roughly understand what the metaverse is. The so-called metaverse is a format where the physical and virtual worlds are connected, communicated, and interconnected under the overlay of multiple cutting-edge technologies.

To achieve this format, more than the current technologies are needed. If the current technologies could support the construction of the metaverse, the metaverse would have already appeared. The current technologies can only support and meet the construction of the mobile internet, and even full video support still needs to be improved, not to mention the virtual and real overlap of the metaverse.

CHAPTER 2

DIGITAL TWIN TECHNOLOGY

2.1 Fields Related to Digital Twin

To clarify the substance and framework of digital twin technology, it is necessary to sort out the fields related to digital twin, as shown in Table 2-1.

Table 2-1   Fields related to digital twin

1	Digital twin and CAD
2	Digital twin and PLM
3	Digital twin and physical entities
4	Digital twin and CPS
5	Digital twin and the cloud
6	Digital twin and Industrial Internet
7	Digital twin and factory production
8	Digital twin and smart manufacturing

(Continued)

9	Digital twin and industrial boundaries
10	Digital twin and CIO

2.1.1   Digital twin and computer-aided design (CAD)

CAD stands for Computer-Aided Design, which emerged in the 1960s as part of an interactive graphics research project proposed by the Massachusetts Institute of Technology. At that time, hardware was expensive and only General Motors and Boeing in the United States used self-developed interactive drawing systems. However, we can also understand CAD as drawing software, although it is more powerful than typical drawing software, as it can create complex engineering diagrams rather than just simple lines or icons. If we need to draw mechanical, architectural, electrical diagrams and other graphics, CAD is the best choice.

A CAD model is formed after CAD is completed. It is static. In most cases, the CAD model is like a pawn in chess, whereas the digital twin is different because it is connected to the production of the physical entity at each step. Before the entity is manufactured, there is no corresponding digital twin, much like a kite flying in the sky is still tethered.

In the past, after a three-dimensional model has fulfilled its purpose, it will be cast aside and lie dormant in a computer folder. On the other hand, digital twins are much more powerful and cannot be underestimated. Based on a high-fidelity, three-dimensional CAD model, a digital twin is given various attributes and functional definitions (including materials, perception systems, machine motion mechanisms, etc.). It is stored in a general graphics database instead of a relational database. It can take in product design, manufacturing, and operational data before injecting them into brand-new product design models that change the design.

What is more noteworthy is that, since the digital twin can have the function of identifying abnormalities in the early stages, product defects can be eliminated prior to production, making it a potential or even realistic substitute for costly but obligatory prototypes.

According to IBM, the digital twin is a digital avatar of a physical entity, which can evolve into a complex ecosystem of interconnected items. It is a dynamic, flesh-

and-blood, and living three-dimensional model. It can be said that the digital twin is an advanced three-dimensional model and an excellent new substitute for physical prototypes. Simply put, a three-dimensional model is the digital representation of a physical object.

2.1.2 Digital twin and PLM

PLM is a new-generation product innovation and collaborative management solution developed after CAD. From the product concept proposal to product information management during its market exit process, PLM has received extensive attention from enterprises. PLM systems can help enterprises establish a unified platform for product R&D design process collaboration and R&D project management, improve R&D efficiency, and enhance product quality. Based on this, PLM gradually expands its business to achieve PLM across front-end planning, R&D design, production and manufacturing, maintenance and repair, shortening product development cycles, enhancing product innovation capabilities, meeting the ever-changing needs of scientific research and manufacturing industries, and improving enterprise core competitiveness.

Therefore, it can be said that PLM is a series of application solutions that can be applied within a single enterprise, across multiple locations, and between enterprises with collaborative relationships in the product development field, supporting the creation, management, distribution, and application of product information throughout its lifecycle. PLM systems can integrate human resources, processes, application systems, and information related to products. PLM is closely related to digital twins.

PLM is something of a misnomer, since post-manufacturing management often ends abruptly, resulting in large amounts of engineering data that were changed during manufacturing but not made known to R&D designers. So, once the product leaves the factory, its current status is no longer known, and it cannot be tracked through PLM.

The emergence of the digital twin has resolved this dilemma. It is a digital representation of the entire lifecycle of physical products (including wear and scrap), making the transparent and automated management of a product throughout its lifecycle a reality. This means that it is only in the era of digital twins that PLM can become a new profit model, achieved through a combination of technologies and business models such as digital twin and the Industrial Internet.

2.1.3   Digital twin and physical entities

Technically digital twins can holographically replicate a physical entity. However, in practice, limited by the depth of a company's definition of product services, it may only encompass some dynamic fragments of physical entities and only solve certain problems. For example, maybe only a few out of the several hundred parts of a machine are used to produce digital twins.

There are three kinds of mappings between digital twins and physical entities:

1)   One-to-one: one machine corresponds to one digital twin.

2)   One-to-many: one digital twin corresponds to multiple meters.

3)   Many-to-one: Several digital twins correspond to one machine.

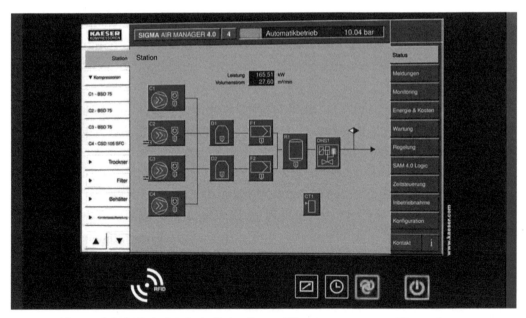

Figure 2-1 A digital twin built by Kaesar Kompressoren and its partners

In some cases, there may be more virtual sensors than physical sensors. As shown in Figure 2-1, Kaesar Kompressoren sells both air compressors and compressed air. The Kaesar Kompressoren air compressor digital twin, established in cooperation with other engineering design software companies, achieves homology between charts and form data. The digital twin can be used for programming and compilation, and through their control of physical entities, the state and operation of physical entities are optimized. So, why is it that only a part, or some key entities, are selected for digital twinning during usage? The core reason lies in cost. To understand this, for example, if we want to create a digital twin of a person, the generated data is extensive, involving significant computational and electrical power consumption, making the cost difficult to bear at this stage.

The metaverse currently requires more work to achieve precisely because of this. We don't need to discuss the metaverse before 2030 because digital twinning technology can only achieve partial dativization.

2.1.4 Digital twin and CPS

A cyber-physical system (CPS) is a complex system that includes computing, networking, and physical entities. Through the organic fusion and deep collaboration of 3C (computing, communication, and control) technologies and human-machine interaction interfaces, CPS technology can remotely, reliably, in real-time, safely, collaboratively, and intelligently control a physical entity in cyberspace. For example, the US Department of Defense has introduced CPS technology from space exploration into the military field. The unmanned combat system can control drones thousands of kilometers away from military bases to conduct reconnaissance and strikes. This is largely due to the CPS technology that the US drone system uses to obtain the necessary ground-to-air information at any time, and the control side of the military base can assess and display the various elements needed for drone reconnaissance and strikes digitally. In short, CPS is a remote and precise control system. It is mainly used to automate unstructured R processes, integrate physical knowledge and models, and shorten cycle time, while also improving product and service quality by implementing self-adaptation and system autoconfiguration.

The digital twin is different from CPS in that it is mainly used for status monitoring and control of physical entities. While processes lie at the heart of digital twin, physical assets are at the core of CPS.

Therefore, we can understand why digital twin technology is combined with CPS. The core is to achieve remote and precise monitoring and control between physical entities and digital twin bodies. From a military perspective, the digital twin system based on CPS technology can achieve precise strikes on remote targets in the digital twin body. This is why the recent precise drone strikes by the United States were based on this kind of technology.

THE DIGITAL TWIN 2.0

To further describe the relationship between these two, it is necessary to discuss another crucial supporting concept of Industry 4.0: Asset Administration Shell (AAS) (Figure 2-2). It enables the data description of physical assets and realizes interaction with other physical assets in the digital space.

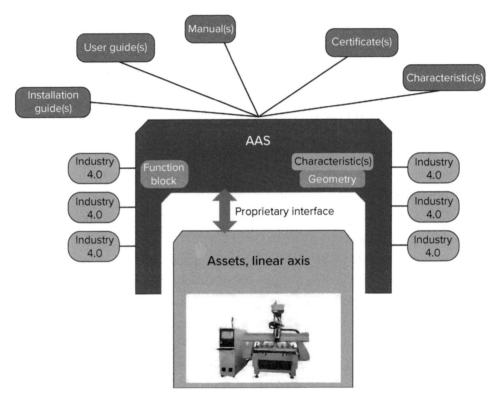

Figure 2-2 AAS

AAS is a software layer that accompanies physical assets, including data and interfaces, and is an important supporting part of the interaction between the physical layer and the cyber layer in CPS. The key points of CPS are cyber, control, and interaction with physical entities. In this sense, the physical layer in CPS must have some kind of programmability—just like the relationship between a digital twin and its corresponding physical entity—and it is realized through digital twin. In the RAMI 4.0 concept of Industry 4.0, physical entities refer to equipment, parts, drawing files, software, etc. But for now, the question of how to implement the digital twin of software, especially how to implement mapping while the software is running, is still unclear.

Analyzing digital twin and the three-layer architecture of CPS studied by Professor Drath from Germany (Figure 2-3), one can see that digital twin is a vital and fundamental element in the construction of CPS. In the future, digital twin and AAS may merge. However, digital twin is not limited to CPS—sometimes it is not used to control processes but only to display status information.

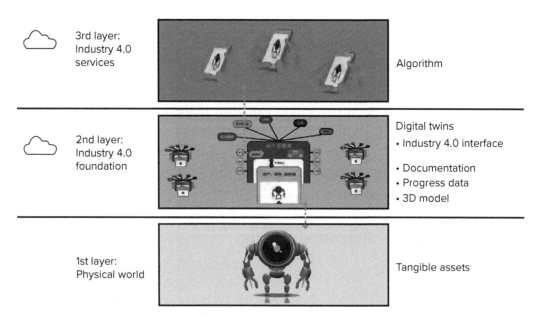

Figure 2-3 The three-layer architecture of CPS and digital twin

2.1.5 Digital twin and the cloud

First, let's look at what the cloud is. "Cloud" refers to a widespread word—"network." In the past, people used the term cloud to refer to the telecommunications network and, later, to refer to the Internet and underlying infrastructure. For example, we used to store data in the space on a USB flash drive, but now, we store data in the cloud. So, the cloud is equivalent to the space on a USB flash drive.

So, what is cloud computing? In the standard definition, cloud computing is a software platform that uses application virtualization technology and integrates various functions such as software search, download, use, management, and backup. Simply put, the cloud is an online server but not a specific server. It could be many servers that are not fixed and may be very large in number. By storing data in the cloud, the possibility of leakage due to lost storage media can be eliminated. In other words, if we lose our USB flash drive, we don't need to worry. We can log in to our account on a new computer, but the data remains.

Siemens' inclination is to view digital twins as purely cloud-based assets because running a digital twin requires great computing resources and flexibility.

SAP's Leonardo platform bought 3D software from a Norwegian company and introduced a cloud solution for digital twins: Predictive Engineering Insights. Using this solution, data about pressure, tension, and materials obtained from sensors can be evaluated, thereby providing enterprises with better insights into their equipment.

GE and Ansys tend to think of digital twin as a hybrid model that includes both edge and cloud computing. An innovative company in the United States developed a software package that builds digital twins catering to edge computing. The difference between this digital twin and the conventional digital twin cloud concept is that it is based on data entered in real time and gradually establishes the concept of machine failure through machine learning. The entire analysis is completed at the edge and does not need to be uploaded to the network (Figure 2-4).

It can be seen that both cloud and offline deployments of digital twins are equally important.

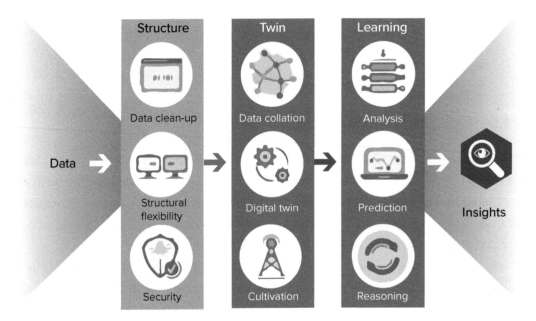

Figure 2-4 The role of digital twin in the conversion of data to knowledge

In my view, in the era of digital twins, there will be a mode of confusion between edge computing and cloud processing. This means that with the advancement of AI chips, especially the implementation of AI-based quantum computing chips, we will be able to directly process a large amount of real-time data at the terminal, and overload processing at the terminal will be shifted to edge collaborative processing. The processing results of these data, or even more complex data processing, will be transmitted to the cloud for processing.

2.1.6 Digital twin and Industrial Internet

From the "Gartner 2017 Hype Cycle for Emerging Technologies" (Figure 2-5), it can be seen that digital twin technology is maturing gradually. In November 2017, IDC announced that by 2020 30% of the world's top 2,000 firms would be using the digital twins of their Industrial Internet products to aid product innovation.

Although it is still too early for the popularization of digital twins, no company can afford to overlook their development. The Industrial Internet is inherently a two-way channel and an incubator for digital twins. It is needed for the collection and exchange of various data from physical entities. The Industrial Internet connects machines and physical infrastructure to digital twins, and places data transmission and storage on the edge or in the cloud, respectively.

It can be said that the Industrial Internet has vitalized digital twin, making it a truly viable model. Digital twin is an important part of the Industrial Internet and at its heart is the ability to make data-based, real-time and correct decisions at the right time and in the right situation, which means customers can be better served. Digital twins are the perfect partners for industrial apps, and a digital twin can support multiple industrial apps. Industrial apps use digital twin technology to analyze a large amount of KPI data, including production efficiency, downtime analysis, failure rate, energy data, and more, to produce evaluation outcomes for feedback and storage so that both product and production modes can be optimized.

2.1.7 Digital twin and factory production

The factory production line refers to the route that the product production process goes through, which is composed of a series of production activities, such as processing, transportation, assembly, inspection, etc., starting from the entry of raw materials into the production site. The workshop production line is organized according to the

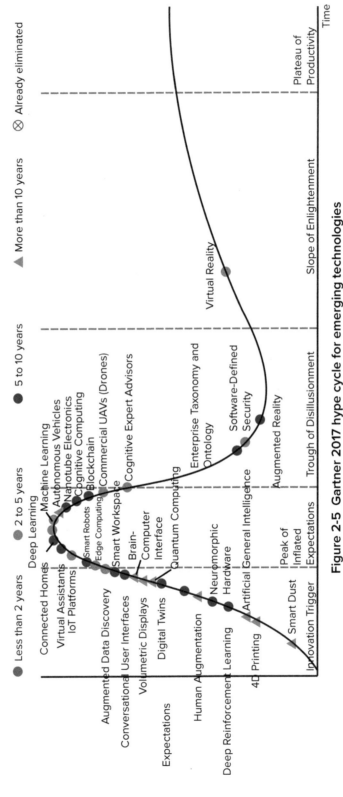

Figure 2-5 Gartner 2017 hype cycle for emerging technologies

object principle, which is a production organization form that completes the product process, that is, according to the product specialization principle, equipped with various equipment and workers necessary for producing a certain product, responsible for completing all manufacturing work of a certain product.

Using digital twins, a large, virtual simulation can be established for machines, production lines, etc. By replicating physical production lines in digital space, the installation, and pilot test processes are simulated in advance. Digital twin records and analyses can be directly copied and used during the installation of the actual production line to greatly lower installation costs and accelerate the birth of new products. At the same time, data fluctuations (such as in energy consumption, error ratio, cycle time, etc.) that are continuously generated during machine commissioning can be used to optimize production, and this data can play a role in subsequent plant and equipment operational processes to raise production efficiency.

Not only can digital twin technology be used in the early stage of factory planning, but it can also be used throughout the entire operation process for full-process supervision, including tracing the trial production process of products. Of course, including energy management, material allocation, and production resource scheduling in the workshop, the digital twin workshop can be the core carrier of an unmanned intelligent workshop.

2.1.8　Digital twin and smart manufacturing

The scope of smart manufacturing is too broad. Digital twin is applicable in smart manufacturing, production, products, and services.

Digital twins are important carriers of smart services. The three relevant types of digital twins are shown in Table 2-2.

Table 2-2　The three types of digital twins

1	Functional Digital Twins
	Indicate the basic status of an object, such as whether a switch is on or off
2	Static Digital Twins
	Collect raw data for subsequent analysis, but no analytical model has been established yet

(Continued)

3	High fidelity Digital Twins Used for in-depth analysis of an entity and to check key factors such as the environment. Used to generate predictions and operational indicators

In the past, once the product was delivered to the user, the company would be free from all responsibility, resulting in a dead end for product development.

Digital twins originate from design, take shape in manufacturing, and finally maintain contact with manufacturers on the user side in the form of services.

Digital twins are indispensable at every stage of smart manufacturing. Currently, through digital twins, R&D personnel can obtain feedback from physical entities and derive the most valuable optimization strategy to maintain a product's popularity. In other words, the digital twin is a "test sandbox," and many new product ideas can be directly transmitted to physical entities through digital twins. Digital twins are gradually becoming the standard for digital enterprises. One example is the German manufacturing company SCHUNK. It will configure a digital twin for each of its 5,000 standard products, of which 50 parts have entered the modeling stage.

2.1.9   Digital twins and industrial boundaries

In the lifecycle of a product, digital twins originate in the creative stage, and the service record of CAD is continuously updated from the beginning, through the realization of physical products and to the consumption stage. However, a product's manufacturing process itself may also be a digital twin. For example, a complex digital twin can be created for process simulation or a manufacturing process to simulate and record real data for interaction.

The same is true for product testing. In the field of automotive autonomous driving, a digital twin used for verifying a level 5 autonomous driving system is a very important application, even if it is not the most complex. Without digital simulation, such verification would require 14 billion kilometers of live testing, making it an immense project with tremendous costs.

For the construction of a factory, digital twins can also play a huge role. Through the building of information models and simulation methods, digital twins are assembled for the plant's water and electricity network, along with various other facilities, in order to achieve a virtual factory assembly. After the factory is completed, these digital twins continue to track and record changes to it.

In terms of digital twin technology in plant facilities and equipment maintenance, Siemens has created digital twins on its COMOS platform with an accompanying mobile app (Figure 2-6). When maintenance workers enter the factory, they can scan any RFID or QR code with their mobile phones to obtain information about spare parts, documents, equipment, and maintenance status before assigning tasks. Similarly, digital twins can be built for rigs, shipping containers, and cargo ships (Figure 2-7).

The actual application of digital twin is much wider than the aforementioned. Digital twins can also take the form of complex organizations or cities—Digital Twin Organization (DTO), also known as Digital Twin Enterprise (DTE). For example, the Dutch software company Mavim provides DTO software that connects physical assets, technology, architecture, infrastructure, customer interactions, business capabilities, strategies, roles, products, services, logistics, and channels within the enterprise to achieve data interconnection and dynamic visualization.

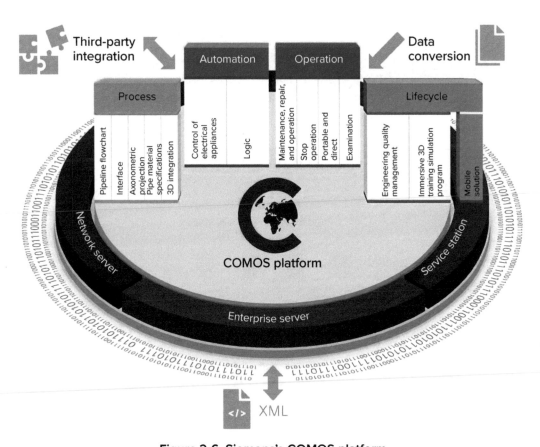

Figure 2-6 Siemens's COMOS platform

Another example is the usage of the 3D Experience City by Dassault Systèmes to create a complete digital twin for urban Singapore (Figure 2-8). Urban planners can then use digital images to better tackle problems in urban energy consumption and traffic; shop owners can then adjust business hours according to human traffic; traffic lights no longer change colors at regular intervals; during emergencies, people can be evacuated using pre-computed models prepared in real time; even the purchasing and distribution relationships between enterprises can be added to form a "virtual social network of enterprises."

Figure 2-7 Digital twins of rigs

Figure 2-8 The digital twin of urban Singapore

In *Ready Player One*, the 2018 movie directed by Steven Spielberg, ordinary people use AR/VR to meet their emotional needs in a virtual city. They can also return to the real community at any time to continue their relationships in the virtual world. All these seem to be increasingly feasible in reality.

2.1.10   Digital twin and the CIO

According to Gartner, 50% of large enterprises will use digital twins by 2021, and the role of the Chief Information Officer (CIO) will be very much in demand. CIOs are senior executives in charge of a company's IT systems, guiding the usage of IT to support the company's goals.

Digital twin focuses on physical assets and new business models centered on assets, while CIOs tend to prioritize process improvement and cost reduction. Whether the CIO can create digital twins independently is an onerous test which goes beyond economic issues to include business models and delivery. For example, when a tire manufacturer delivers a tire to a user, it must also deliver a set of digital twins and supporting software at the same time. This means that software delivery and data delivery clauses will appear in the business contract, making this a business issue that goes beyond corporate informatization.

In addition to the need for various departments in the company to jointly develop strategies, there are many digital ethical issues that require the enterprise to look at the possible outcomes with partners and users. Obviously, the digital twins of an enterprise will affect suppliers and partners. These are not matters that the CIO can handle alone.

2.2   The Digital Twin Technological System

The realization of digital twin technology depends on the development and application of many advanced technologies. From the bottom up, its technological system can be divided into a data collection layer, a data assurance layer, a modeling computation layer, a function layer, an immersive experience layer, and an application layer at the top. Starting from the modeling computation layer, each layer is based on the previous, enriching and expanding on the previous. Figure 2-9 shows the digital twin technological system.

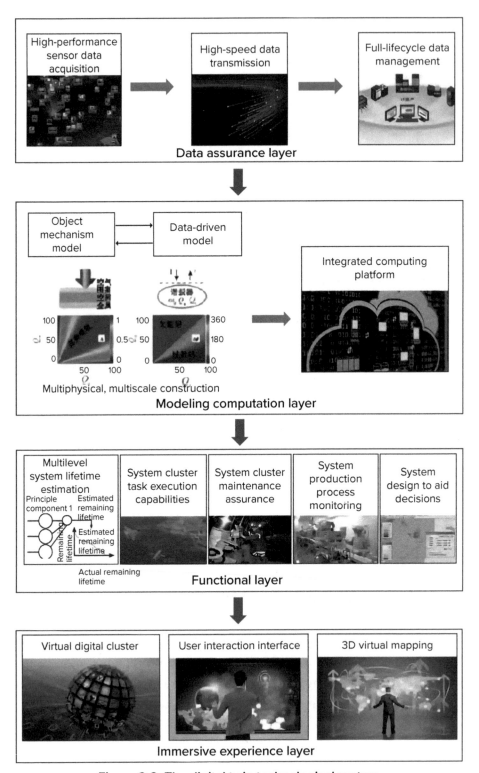

Figure 2-9 The digital twin technological system

2.2.1 Data assurance layer

The data assurance layer is the foundation of the digital twin technological system and supports the operation of its upper layers. It comprises three parts: high-performance sensor data collection, high-speed data transmission, and full-lifecycle data management.

Advanced sensor technology and distributed sensing technology provide the digital twin technological system with more accurate and adequate data-source support. Data is the base of the digital twin technological system. Massive amounts of complex system operational data include the most important information used to extract and build system features. Compared to expert experience, the real-time sensor information of the system is more accurate, reflects real-time physical characteristics of the system, and is more applicable to systems with multiple operating stages. As the frontline of the entire system, its importance is beyond doubt.

The adoption of high-bandwidth optical fiber technology means that the transmission of massive amounts of sensor data is no longer limited by bandwidth. As the amount of data collected from complex industrial systems is humongous, the increased bandwidth shortens the time required for systems to transmit data, thereby reducing system delays, guaranteeing both the real-time nature of the system and real-time tracking by its digital twin(s).

The development of distributed cloud server storage technology provides a platform guarantee for full-lifecycle data storage and management. The high-efficiency storage structure and data retrieval structure provide an important guarantee for the storage and rapid extraction of massive amounts of historical operating data, thus providing a technological system which is based on cloud storage and cloud computing with a base of historical data, enabling the quick and reliable completion of the data query and retrieval stages of Big Data analysis and computation.

2.2.2 Modeling computation layer

Digital twin is an advanced, integrated, and systematic technology. Only by understanding this concept can we truly grasp the essence of digital twin. For example, what is the metaverse? When we say the metaverse is the future, what exactly does it refer to? It represents a future social form. This future social form is based on a technological system. Just like the era we are in today, known as the Internet era, is because there is a core technological system behind this era, which is dominated by the Internet.

Steve Jobs once used a famous "necklace" metaphor. Apple's introduction of the iPhone connected multiple single-point technologies, such as a multi-touch screen, iOS system, high-resolution camera, and large-capacity battery. It redefined smartphones and ushered in the booming mobile internet era for over a decade. Apple's iPhone was the pioneer of smartphones, introducing touchscreen functionality. The iPhone 3GS ushered in the 3G era and introduced the App Store ecosystem. The iPhone 4s debuted the voice assistant Siri, leading the development of voice technology on smartphones. The iPhone 5 series introduced Touch ID, leading fingerprint recognition technology. The iPhone 6 series introduced Face ID and the iPhone 8 series replaced Touch ID with Face ID, bringing about full-screen technology. We can see that behind a consumer-grade iPhone is a whole technological system, where each technology is indispensable, and any single technology alone cannot create an iPhone. In other words, the iPhone is the sum of a series of "connecting the dots" technological innovations.

Similarly, behind the era of digital twin is a technological system called digital twin. Therefore, digital twin is not just a single technology, but a technological system. This technological system is a systematic architecture. For example, digital twin is an innovative application that integrates and combines a series of technologies such as perception, transmission, computation, modeling, and simulation. Its architectural layers include data assurance, modeling and computation, functional, and immersive experience layers. The implementation of each layer is built upon the functionalities of the previous layers, enriching and expanding the capabilities of the preceding layers. The following figure illustrates the technological system of digital twin (see Figure 2-9).

If we delve into the details of these functionalities, we will discover an extensive and complex system, similar to how we use smartphones and mobile internet today. While we interact with the phone screen through simple operations, there is a complex and vast technological system behind it. For example, in the modeling layer, the key technology of digital twin lies in the construction of models. It involves using digital technology to build a multidimensional model, namely the digital twin. From the perspective of the modeling layer, the digital twin can be categorized into types such as geometric, physical, and rule-based models.

It can be said that the integration of technologies has contributed to the birth of digital twin. In comparison to other individual digital technologies, digital twin exhibits five key characteristics: interoperability, scalability, real-time capability, fidelity, and closed-loop functionality. These characteristics ultimately converge to form the advantages of digital twin technology. Today, thanks to the development of new-generation information technologies such as the IoT, big data, cloud computing, and artificial intelligence, the implementation of digital twin has entered the fast lane and is gradually being applied in various fields, such as manufacturing, transportation, and healthcare. The advancement of cutting-edge technologies like the IoT and big data has broken down data silos, enabling the rapid transfer of data from the physical world to the digital twin world, and facilitating rapid optimization and feedback in the digital realm.

Digital twin has become an inevitable outcome and a necessary path toward digitization. The emphasis of digital twin on the one-to-one mapping with the real world and real-time interaction in the virtual world will increasingly be integrated into society's production and daily life. It helps achieve precise control over the real world, reduces operational costs, and enhances management efficiency.

2.2.3 Functional layer

The functional layer provides corresponding functions for system design, production, usage, and maintenance, including multilevel system lifetime estimation, evaluation of the system cluster's ability to execute tasks, system cluster maintenance guarantee, system production process monitoring, system design auxiliary decision-making, etc. Taking aim at abnormalities and degradation in the usage of complex systems, the degradation modeling and lifetime estimation of key components and subsystems of the system are carried out at the functional layer to provide guidance and evaluation basis for the management of system health. For complex system clusters that need to work together, the functional layer provides them with task-executability evaluations and self-perceptiveness to aid decision-making during the execution of collaborative tasks. Based on the deep self-perceptiveness of each entity in the system cluster, cluster-based system maintenance guarantee can be further implemented according to the system health status, saving on system maintenance expenses and avoiding human resource wastage, and achieving batch maintenance guarantee in the system cluster.

The ultimate goal of the digital twin technological system is to achieve system design and production process optimization and improvement based on the full-lifecycle health status of the system, so that after the design and production stages are completed, the system can perform well throughout its lifecycle.

As the direct value manifestation of the digital twin system, the functional layer can be customized according to actual system needs. Based on the powerful information interface provided by the modeling computation layer, the functional layer can fulfill the multiple performance indicators of reliability, accuracy, real-time performance, and intelligent decision-making, thus improving product performance throughout the entire lifecycle.

2.2.4 Immersive experience layer

The immersive experience layer is mainly to provide users with a good environment for human-computer interaction, so that users enjoy an immersive technical experience, thereby quickly understanding and mastering the characteristics and functions of complex systems. This would allow the users to easily use voice and gestures to access information in the functional layer and receive information support for analysis and decision-making. The usage of future technological systems will no longer be limited to audio and visual, but will also integrate information and sensing of touch, pressure, body movements, and gravity so that users are given realistic system scenarios. Through AI, users can also understand and learn about the system attributes and features that cannot be reflected in such scenarios.

Users can obtain a deeper understanding of system scenarios by learning about and understanding physical quantities and model analysis outcomes that are not accessible or cannot be collected from physical objects. This would inspire users and allow them to verify their inspirations in design, production, usage, and maintenance.

Users are in direct contact with the immersive experience layer, so its usability and interactivity are important indicators. Figure 2-10 is taken from NASA's technology roadmap. Taking the integration of technology in digital twins as an example, the broad development prospects of digital twin technology is described, focusing on fulfilling the technical requirements related to extreme reliability, so that the technology is integrated into actual projects and continues to develop.

The immersive experience layer integrates multiple advanced technologies to achieve multiphysical and multiscale cluster simulation. It uses high-fidelity modeling, simulation technology, state-depth perception, and self-learning technology to build a virtual real-time task twin of the target system to continuously predict system health, remaining service life, and task execution success probability. Digital clusters are important examples of the progress in digital twin implementation in actual projects. This is of great significance for the future execution of high-reliability tasks in cost-controllable situations.[1]

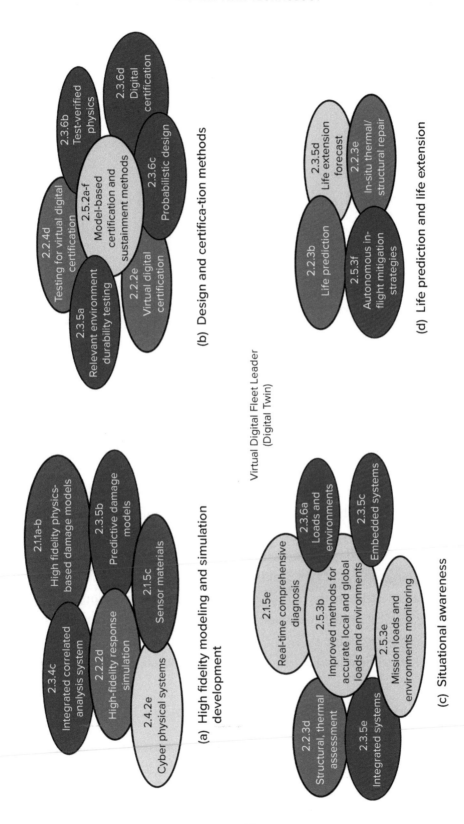

Figure 2-10 Integration of technology in digital twins

2.3   The Core Technology of Digital Twins

There are six aspects to the core technology behind digital twins, as shown in Table 2-3.

Table 2-3   The core technology of digital twins

1	Multidomain and multiscale fusion modeling
2	Datadriven and physical model fusion status assessment
3	Data collection and transmission
4	Lifecycle data management
5	VR rendering
6	Highperformance computing

2.3.1   Multidomain and multiscale fusion modeling

At present, most modeling methods involve the development and maturation of models in specific fields. Following this, integration and data fusion methods are then used to integrate independent models from different domains into a comprehensive system-level model. Such integration lacks depth and cohesion.

Multidomain modeling refers to the implementation of cross-domain design understanding and modeling of physical systems from different domains and deep mechanism levels from the initial conceptual design stage.

The difficulty of multidomain modeling is that the fusion of multiple characteristics will result in a large degree of freedom in the system equations. At the same time, to ensure the dynamic update of the model based on high-precision sensor measurements, the collected data must be highly consistent with the actual system data. In general, the difficulties are reflected in the three aspects of length, time scale, and coupling range. Overcoming these difficulties will help build a more accurate digital twin system.

2.3.2   Data-driven and physical model fusion status assessment

For a digital twin target system with complicated mechanism(s) and structure(s), it is often difficult to establish an accurate and reliable system-level physical model. Therefore, using the analytical physical model of the target system alone is insufficient for evaluating the state of the system or producing the best evaluation outcome. In comparison, data-driven methods use the system's historical and real-time operating data to update, modify, connect, and supplement the physical model, fully integrating the characteristics of the system's mechanism(s) and operating data. This allows better integration with the system's real-time operating status to obtain an evaluation system that dynamically tracks the status of the target system in real time.

At present, there are two main methods of combining data-driven methods with physical models.

1) Data-driven methods are used to modify the parameters of the analytical physical model.
2) The analytical physical model and data-driven methods are used in parallel, and a final evaluation result is obtained after weighing the reliability of both outputs.

However, both methods lack deeper-level integration and optimization and have insufficient knowledge of the system mechanism and data characteristics. A deeper understanding and consideration of system characteristics is required during integration. Currently, the obstacle to integrating models and data lies in their integration and complementarity at the theoretical level. How to go about reasonably and effectively combining the statistical characteristics of high-precision sensor data with the system's mechanism model, in order to obtain better status evaluation and monitoring outcomes, is an issue that needs to be considered and resolved urgently.

The inability to effectively combine physical models and data-driven ones is also reflected in the fact that full-lifecycle statuses cannot be shared between existing complex industrial systems and equipment systems; multisource and heterogeneous lifecycle data cannot be effectively integrated, and optimism for digital twin rests mostly on high-complexity and high-performance algorithms such as machine learning and deep learning.

Increasingly, industrial condition-monitoring data or mathematical models are replacing physical models that are difficult to construct, but at the same time, there are still problems to tackle, such as the difficulty of describing the process or mechanism of the target system, and the limited performance of the digital twin systems constructed.

Therefore, effectively enhancing or integrating digital design and simulation, virtual modeling, process simulation, etc., in the early stages of complex equipment or industrial systems, and further considering the composition of complex systems and simulation modeling of factors such as operational mechanism, signal flow, interface coupling, etc., are bottlenecks that need to be overcome in building digital twin systems.

2.3.3   Data collection and transmission

The collection and rapid transmission of data from high-precision sensors forms the basis of the entire digital twin system. The sensors need to be at an optimal state in terms of temperature, pressure, and vibration to reproduce the operating state of the target system. The distribution of sensors and the construction of sensor networks are based on the principles of speed, safety, and accuracy. The system state is characterized by various physical quantities from the distributed-sensor information-collection system. At the same time, it is very important to build a fast and reliable information transmission network so that system state information can be securely sent to computers for further processing.

The digital twin system is a real-time, dynamic, hyper-realistic mapping of the physical system. The collection, transmission, and updating of data in real time is crucial to digital twins. A large number of high-precision sensors of various types is distributed across the frontline of the digital twin system to fulfill the most basic sensory role.

At present, the problem with data acquisition for digital twin systems is that the type, precision, reliability, operating environment, etc., of the sensors are limited by existing sensor technology, which restricts the available methods of data collection. While real-time and secure data transmission is key, the technical levels of existing network transmission equipment and network structure are unable to support higher transmission rates. Sufficient attention should also be given to network security in practical applications.

With the rapid improvement of sensors, many micro-electro-mechanical system (MEMS) sensors are becoming more cost-effective and highly integrated. At the same time, the increasing usage of high-bandwidth and low-cost wireless transmission technologies such as the IoT allows more complex states such as anomalies, failures, and degradations to be captured in order to characterize and evaluate the target system operating state. This is especially the case for aging complex equipment or industrial systems with poorer sensing abilities still far from having CPS.

Many new sensing methods or modules are compatible with or can be built into, existing object-system systems to form low-cost systems or platforms that combine sensing, data acquisition, and data transmission. This is also a key support for digital twin.

2.3.4 Lifecycle data management

The full-lifecycle data storage and management of complex systems is an important support for digital twin systems. The use of cloud servers—for the distributed management of a system's massive volume of operational data, the high-speed reading of data and production of secure backup copies, and the provision of reliable data for the data intelligent-analysis algorithm—plays an important role in the operation of the digital twin system. Storing data from the entire lifecycle of a system provides more adequate information for data analysis and display, allowing the system to support historical status playback, structural health degradation analysis, and intelligent analytical functions for any historical point.

Massive historical operational data also provides a wealth of sample information for data mining. By extracting effective features in the data and analyzing the correlation between data, a lot of unknown but potentially valuable information can be obtained to deepen the understanding of the system mechanism and data characteristics, so as to produce a hyper-realistic digital twin. As research advances, full lifecycle data will continue to be a reliable data source and key support.

Distributed servers with spare storage are needed for full lifecycle data storage and management. Since digital twin systems have high requirements for real-time data, one challenge is optimizing the data distribution structure, storage method, and retrieval method to obtain real-time and reliable data-read. In particular, data security for enterprises and information protection for equipment must be considered. Currently, a more feasible technical solution is a data center or data management system with a secure private cloud as the core.

2.3.5 VR rendering

VR technology can present the system's manufacturing, operational, and maintenance status in a hyper-realistic form, conduct multidomain and multiscale status monitoring and evaluation of every subsystem in a complex system, and attach intelligent monitoring and analysis outcomes to each sub-system and component. At the same time that the physical system is replicated, virtual mapping is used to superimpose the digital analysis results onto the digital system to provide an immersive visual, audio, and tactile VR experience for real-time, continuous human-computer interaction. VR technology can help users quickly understand and learn about the target system's principle(s), structure(s), characteristic(s), change(s), health, status, etc., through its digital twin. It can also inspire users to improve the design and manufacture of the target system, and provide inspiration for optimization and innovation. Through simple actions, users can access the different levels of the system's structure and status. This is especially significant for monitoring and guiding the manufacturing, safe operation, and condition-based maintenance of complex equipment, providing more information and options than the physical system.

The technical difficulty with VR technology is that a large number of high-precision sensors are needed to collect the operating data of the system to provide the necessary data sources and support for VR technology. At the same time, the technical bottleneck of VR technology also needs to be overcome to provide a more realistic VR experience.

In addition, in industrial data analysis, research and application of data presentation are often neglected. As data analysis tasks become more complex, and to cope with the needs of high-dimensional and real-time data modeling and analysis, more attention should be given to data presentation technology. This is an important link to support the construction of digital twin systems.

At present, many Internet companies are constantly launching data presentation spaces and launching or upgrading data presentation software. Industrial data analysis can borrow from such data presentation technologies to enhance the performance and effectiveness of data analysis visualization.

2.3.6   High-performance computing

The complex functions of digital twin systems largely depend on their computing platforms. Real-time performance is an important performance indicator. Therefore, a cloud server platform based on distributed computing is vital. Optimizing data and algorithm structures is important for improving task execution speed to ensure the real-time nature of the system. It is vital for the application of the digital twin to comprehensively consider the performance of the computing platform, the time delay of the data transmission network, and the computing power of the cloud computing platform, as well as how to design the optimal system computing architecture to meet the real-time analysis and computing requirements of the system. As the computing base of the entire system, the platform's computing power directly determines overall system performance.

The real-time nature of digital twin systems means that extremely high computing performance is required, so computing platforms need to be improved and computing structures optimized. Presently, the computing performance of the system is still limited by these two aspects, so more efforts should be made to achieve breakthroughs in these two areas to better serve the development of digital twin technology.

Moving high-performance data-analysis algorithms into the cloud and heterogeneous accelerated-computing systems (such as CPU-GPU or CPU-FPGA) can be considered on the basis of existing cloud computing since they can meet the requirements of real-time, high-performance computing in industrial scenarios.[2]

2.4 Creating Digital Twins

Digital twins can bring real value to companies, create new sources of income, and help companies solve important strategic problems. As the technology develops and provides increased flexibility and reduced costs, companies can create digital twins to generate value in a shorter period of time even with a smaller investment. Digital twin applications come in various forms throughout the product lifecycle. They can resolve in real time problems that could not be solved in the past and create value that was not even imaginable just a few years before. The real question for companies may not be whether they should deploy digital twins but where to start doing so, how to get the most value in the shortest time, and how to stand out from the competition.

2.4.1 Two key points in creating digital twins

The two key points in creating digital twins are shown in Table 2-4, i.e., process design and information requirements and the conceptual architecture.

Table 2-4 Two key points in creating digital twins

1	Process design and information requirements From asset design to its actual usage and maintenance
2	Conceptual architecture Create enabling technology and integrate real assets and their digital twins to enable the real-time flow of sensor data to make operational and transaction information the core systems of enterprises

2.4.1.1 Process design and information requirements

Process design takes place before a digital twin is created. Standard process design techniques are utilized to show how business processes, process managers, business applications, information, and physical assets interact. They are also used to create relevant diagrams and connect production processes with applications, data requirements, and the types of sensor information needed to create digital twins.

A variety of features in process design will be enhanced to improve cost, time, and asset efficiency. These form the basis of digital twins, and enhancing their effectiveness begins here.

2.4.1.2 Conceptual architecture

By creating enabling technology, and integrating real assets and their digital twins to enable the real-time flow of sensor data and operational and transaction information form the core systems of enterprises. The conceptual architecture of the digital twin can be divided into six easy-to-understand steps (Figure 2-11).[3]

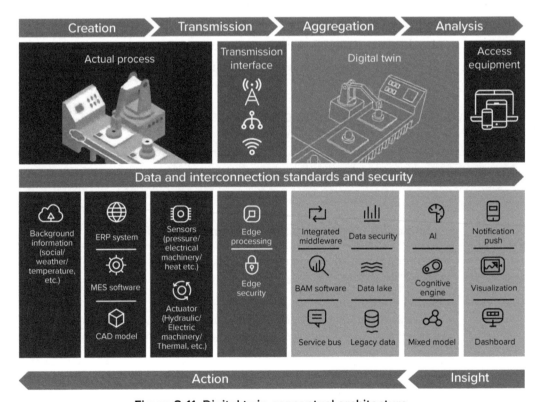

Figure 2-11 Digital twin conceptual architecture

1) Creation. This step includes equipping the physical process with a large number of sensors to detect and acquire key data about the physical process and its environment. The data detected by the sensors is converted into protected digital information by the encoder and transmitted to the digital twin system. Sensor signals can be enhanced with process-oriented information from manufacturing systems, ERP systems, CAD models, and supply chain systems, providing the digital twin system with a large amount of continuously updated data for analysis.

2) Transmission. Network transmission is one of the major changes that make digital twins a reality, and it contributes to the seamless and real-time two-way integration/interconnection between actual processes and digital platforms. The transmission includes the following three major components.

   First, edge processing. The edge interface connects sensors and historical process databases, so that signals and data are processed near their sources and transmits the data to the platform. This helps to convert proprietary protocols into easier-to-understand data formats and reduce network transmission volume.

   Second, transmission interface. The transmission interface transfers the information acquired by sensors to the integration function.

   Third, edge security. The most commonly used security measures include firewalls, application keys, encryption, and device certificates.

3) Aggregation. In the aggregation, obtained data is stored in a repository and processed prior to analysis. Data aggregation and processing can be done in-situ or in the cloud.

4) Analysis. In the analysis step, the data is analyzed and processed for visualization. Data scientists and analysts can use advanced data-analysis platforms and technologies to develop iterative models to uncover insights, make recommendations, and guide the decision-making process.

5) Insights. In this step, insights uncovered by analysis tools will be presented in the dashboard as a visual chart, highlighting unacceptable differences in performance between the digital twin model and the physical world analogues in one or more dimensions, indicating areas that possibly need to be investigated or replaced.

6) Action. In this step, actionable insights formed in the previous steps are fed back to the physical assets and digital processes to fulfill the function of the digital twin. After the insights are decoded, they are relayed to actuators responsible for movement or mechanism control or are used to update back-end systems that control the supply chain and order-placing behavior. Manual interventions are allowed, thus completing the last rung of the closed loop between the physical world and the digital twin.

It should be noted that the above-mentioned conceptual architecture should have flexibility and scalability in various aspects, such as analysis, processing, sensor quantity, and information. In so doing, the architecture can then develop rapidly, even in a market environment that changes exponentially.

2.4.2 How to create and deploy digital twins

In creating a digital twin, one of the biggest challenges lies in determining the optimal solution for the digital twin model. Too simple a model would cause the digital twin to fall short of its expected value, whereas being too fixated on speed and wide coverage would entail dealing with the myriad technologies behind sensors, sensor signals, and model-building. Therefore, companies need to find the right balance to move forward. Figure 2-12 is a schematic diagram of a suitably complex digital twin initial-deployment model.[4]

2.4.2.1 Think of the possibilities

Imagine and select a series of solutions that can reap the benefits of digital twin. Although the applicable solution(s) depends on the company and operating environment, they usually have the following two important characteristics.

First, the envisioned product or production process is extremely valuable to the enterprise, so investing in the creation of a digital twin is absolutely necessary.

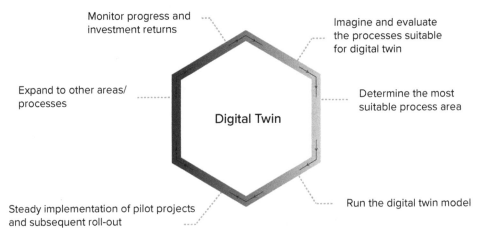

Figure 2-12 Schematic diagram of a suitably complex digital twin initial-deployment model

Second, there are some unknown process(es) or product problems that are not yet clear, and addressing these is expected to create value for customers or the enterprise.

2.4.2.2 Evaluation
Every solution is evaluated to determine the process in which digital twin can be used to quickly achieve results. One way to go about this is to hold a meeting for leaders of the operations, business, and technical departments to conduct a joint evaluation.

2.4.2.3 Determine the process
Identify the digital twin model with the highest potential value and probability of success for the trial. Comprehensively consider operational, commercial, and organizational-change management factors to create the best operational plan for the trial. At the same time, focus on areas that are likely to expand in terms of equipment, site-selection, or technological scale.

2.4.2.4 Commission the project
Through agile iteration, quickly put the project into trial operation to speed up the learning process and maximize the return on investment through effective risk management. During the trial, the implementation team must remain adaptable and open-minded to create an open ecosystem that is still undetermined. Depending on the prevailing trends, the system can integrate new data and accept new technologies or partners.

2.4.2.5 Formally roll out the process
After a successful trial existing tools, technologies, and scripts can be used to formally roll out the digital twin development and deployment process. This includes integrating the various scattered implementation processes of the company, setting up data lakes, improving performance and productivity, improving governance, and standardizing data. It also involves advancing structural changes in the organization to provide support for digital twin.

2.4.2.6 Expand the scale of digital twin
After a successful rollout, the next step is to focus on opportunities to expand the scale of digital twin. The targets would be similar processes and those related to the trial. Drawing on the experience of the trial, the same tools, technologies, and scripts are used to rapidly scale up.

2.4.2.7 Monitoring and testing

Monitor the solution and objectively assess the value generated by the digital twin. Determine whether tangible benefits are generated during the cycle: improved productivity, quality, and utilization rates or reduced incidents and costs. Constantly debug the digital twin process and observe the outcome to determine the best configuration.

More importantly, unlike conventional projects working with digital twins is a continuous process. Enterprises that wish to hold a unique market advantage for the long term need to continue exploring the use of digital twin in new business areas.

All in all, for a company to be successful in the early stage of its digital twin journey, it must be able to formulate and execute the digital twin plan, while ensuring that its digital twin generates value for the company. To do so, the entire company needs to embrace digital technology and digital twin, including the R&D and sales departments. It should also use digital twin to change its business model and decision-making process so as to continuously open up new sources of income.

2.5   The Nine Key Elements That Determine Digital Twin

Digital twin is the future, it is a trend, and this is a consensus that does not require discussion or debate. Simply put, digital twin is the interconnection, intercommunication, and interaction between the virtual and physical real world. To effectively overlay the virtual and physical worlds in this social form, nine key elements are crucial in this development process: hardware, connectivity, computing power, interaction, platforms, standards, payments, content, and rules.

Hardware: It is easily understood that humans and objects must be digitized to achieve data integration. This inevitably requires hardware such as smart wearables and intelligent sensors, including hardware support for presentation and interaction technologies.

Connectivity: To interconnect, intercommunicate, and interact between the virtual and physical entities, and to overlay these two worlds, it is essential to establish connectivity. Therefore, connectivity technology is of great importance for connecting the virtual and real worlds and connecting various ecosystems and applications within this new form.

Computing Power: This is a topic I often discuss. One key technology is computing power to realize the digital twin world or create the appearance of the metaverse. The current technology cannot support the enormous amount of data generated by various interactions between the virtual and physical realms. Solving the computing power issue will not rely on current computer technology but will require implementing quantum computing technology.

Interaction: Since we are in the digital twin world, where the physical and virtual worlds are interconnected, intercommunicated, and interacted, good interaction technology is needed to support this interaction process. Currently, whether it is VR, AR, MR, or XR, interaction is one of the challenging technologies. We are unable to provide efficient and immersive interaction technology, and this type of interaction technology will ultimately depend on the development of the smart wearables industry.

Platforms: Once the digital twin Earth enters a mature stage, various applications and platforms will inevitably emerge. Among them, platforms will be built based on national entities, and various independent application innovation platforms will be derived from them. This is also why countries are paying attention to and promoting this concept. Behind the digital twin earth or the digital twin world is a civilization, culture, and value system. The question of who will lead the construction of such platforms is worth paying attention to.

Standards: Ultimately, digital twin will still form a new form of centralization based on decentralized technology, but this form of centralization will be more open compared to the current centralization. This decentralized technology ultimately requires the unified recognition of countries worldwide and the establishment of governance and construction based on these standards. Therefore, these standards are the key focus and the basis for countries to seize and participate in the discourse and construction of digital twin.

Payments: Where there is connectivity, there will be transactions, and where there are transactions, there is a need for payments. Therefore, in the world of digital twin, seamless intercommunication and exchange of payment methods between the virtual and physical realms are crucial. This payment method may not necessarily be based on digital currency; it could be a new information exchange or transfer form.

Content: The metaverse is based on digital twin technology and incorporates more entertainment elements, and these entertainment or lifestyle elements will construct a new form of business. The emergence of any platform or form ultimately translates into commercial transactions through content. For this reason, we are seeing the emergence of virtual houses, virtual sand, virtual characters, virtual bricks, and more on current virtual platforms. However, with the further development of digital twin or the metaverse based on digital twin, more virtual content will emerge in virtual platform spaces, continuously enriching the virtual world's life.

Rules: In current applications of digital twin, they are either based on standards, rules, or processes for construction. However, with the addition of lifestyle elements, expanding personalized virtual life and socialization methods will inevitably pose new demands on rules. In the virtual world, including digitized virtual characters, various orderly behavioral norms have not been established, resulting in "crimes" that cannot be implemented in the real world within this space. Therefore, rules will be the next focus to support the development of digital twin in constructing the metaverse and enabling the application of artificial intelligence.[5]

CHAPTER 3

DIGITAL TWIN AND INDUSTRY 4.0

After the Internet became a daily application, the industrial sector, under the influence of Internet technology and driven by technologies such as the miniaturization of chips and sensors, began to draw attention to the Industrial Internet. In major industrial countries such as China, the United States, Germany, and Japan, the revolution of the Industrial Internet, or the technological transformation of Industry 4.0, has been elevated to the level of the national strategy to varying degrees. This has prompted both industries and capital to contemplate the direction of the Industrial Internet's transformation, naturally focusing on the more advanced technology of digital twin, which enables virtual and physical interconnection, communication, and interaction.

Therefore, the revolution of Industry 4.0 catalyzes digital twin technology. However, it does not mean that digital twin is generated based on the concept of Industry 4.0. Instead, it leverages the wave of the industrial revolution to bring advanced military technologies into civilian fields. As a result, digitalized factories and workshops based on digital twin technology have gained attention and are being established and applied. With the advent of smart manufacturing, the term "digital twin" has been given greater exposure to become an extremely important technical component in the journey toward Industry 4.0.

3.1 The Product Digital Twin

3.1.1 Definition

After taking into account the evolution process and the relevant explanations of existing product digital twins, one can define the product digital twin in the following way:

It is a reconstruction and digital mapping of the essential elements in the work state and progress of physical product entities in the information space. It is a multiphysical, multiscale, hyper-realistic, and dynamic-probability simulation model that can be used to simulate, monitor, diagnose, predict, and control the formation, state, and behavior of physical product entities in the real world.

The product digital twin is based on the product model generated in the design stage. In the subsequent manufacturing and service stages, the interaction of data and information with the physical product entity is used to constantly improve its integrity and accuracy. Finally, a complete and accurate digital description of the physical product entity is produced. Some scholars have also called digital twins "digital mirrors" or "digital mappings."

Based on this definition, the content of a product digital twin can be seen in see Table 3-1.

Table 3-1   The connotation of product digital twin

1	The product digital twin is an integrated simulation model of physical product entities in the information space. It is a full-lifecycle digital archive of physical product entities which enables the unified integrated management of product lifecycle data and value chain data.
2	The continuous interaction of data and information with the physical product entity is used to constantly improve the product digital twin.
3	Its final form is a complete and accurate digital description of the physical product entity.
4	It can be used to simulate, monitor, diagnose, predict, and control the formation and state of physical product entities in the real world.

Product digital twins go far beyond the definition of digital prototypes (or virtual prototypes) and digital products. They do not merely describe the product's geometry, function, and performance, but also other formation processes and states in the manufacturing and maintenance stages. A digital prototype (or virtual prototype) refers to a digital description of the entire machine or a subsystem with independent functions. It not only reflects the geometric properties of the product, but also its function and performance in at least one area. It is formed in the product design stage and can be applied throughout the product lifecycle, for instance in engineering design, manufacturing, assembly, inspection, sales, use, after-sales, and recycling.

In contrast, digital products refer to activities that digitally describe the function, performance, and physical characteristics of mechanical products.

Digital prototypes and digital products are mainly concerned with describing the geometry, function, and performance of the product design stage and do not describe the formation processes and states during other stages of the product lifecycle, like the manufacturing and maintenance stages.[13]

3.1.2 The four basic functions of the product digital twin

The basic functions of product digital twins are modeling, monitoring and manipulating, diagnostics, and prognostics. The higher the level of the digital twin, the higher the requirement for its functions (Figure 3-1).

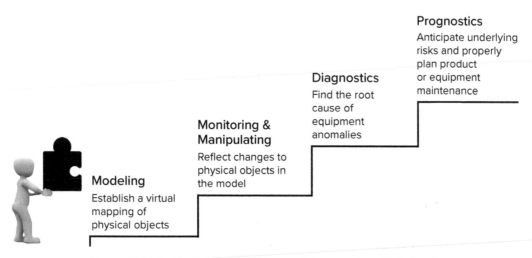

Figure 3-1 The four basic functions of the product digital twin

3.1.2.1 Modeling

Modeling means establishing a virtual mapping of physical objects. Modeling is the lowest level of digital twin technology and mainly involves establishing a 3D model of the actual model and using assembly, animation, and other methods to simulate the movement of parts. For example, through the establishment of a digital 3D model, we can see the digital changes of every part, circuit, joint, and other aspects of the engine during a car's operation for preventive maintenance.

3.1.2.2 Monitoring and manipulating

Monitoring and manipulating refers to reflecting changes to physical objects in their virtual models. Digital twins can be used to monitor and operate equipment, connect the physical model to the virtual model, and reflect changes in the physical objects through their virtual models. For example, each device in a factory of the future will have a digital twin, through which we can accurately understand how these physical devices operate. Through the seamless matching of digital models and physical equipment, operating data of the equipment monitoring system can be obtained in real time, thereby pre-empting faults and providing timely maintenance.

Monitoring is only a taste of what digital twin technology offers; its ultimate application is control. Through digital models, remote control of equipment will become possible in the future, and terms like "remote assistance," "remote operation," and "remote emergency commands" will become commonplace in the daily management of enterprises.

3.1.2.3 Diagnostics

Digital twins can be used to find the root cause of equipment anomalies. The difference between monitoring versus diagnostics/prognostics is that monitoring allows control inputs to be adjusted to obtain a system response, but the system design cannot be changed during the process, while diagnostics/prognostics/prediction allows design inputs to be adjusted.

For example, CnTech developed a vehicle drivability evaluation system. During the test, the system will score the vehicle's performance in the simulation model based on the various signals from sensors installed in the car. The score is then used to judge the comfort of the ride (Figure 3-2). Through this objective evaluation method, evaluation differences caused by the subjectivity of human assessors are avoided.

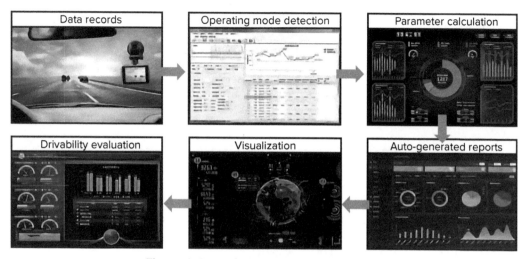

Figure 3-2 Vehicle drivability diagnostics

3.1.2.4 Prognostics

Prognostics occupies the highest level of digital twin technology, which can help companies predict potential risks and rationally plan future products or equipment maintenance.

Currently, major enterprises are using predictive product repair and maintenance widely. For example, GE produces a digital twin for every engine, turbine, and nuclear magnetic resonance device. These digital models are then debugged and tested in virtual reality. To maximize machine efficiency, all it takes is to apply the optimized scheme to the actual model.[14] Through digital twin technology, enterprises can plan their products carefully to avoid wasting a lot of time and money on physical product verification.

3.1.3   The basic characteristics of product digital twins

The main characteristics of product digital twins are shown in Table 3-2.

Table 3-2   The main characteristics of product digital twins

Virtual	Dynamic
Unique	Hyper-realistic

(Continued)

Multiphysical	Computable
Multiscale	Probabilistic
Hierarchical	Multidisciplinary
Integrated	

3.1.3.1 *Virtual*

The product digital twin is a virtual or digital mapping model of actual products in the information space. It resides in the information space (or virtual space) and not in the physical space.

3.1.3.2 *Unique*

A physical product corresponds to a product digital twin.

3.1.3.3 *Multiphysical*

The product digital twin is a digital mapping of physical products based on their physical characteristics. It not only needs to describe the product's geometry (such as shape, size, tolerance, etc.), but also other physical characteristics such as its structural dynamic model, thermodynamics model, stress analysis model, fatigue damage model, and material characteristics, such as stiffness, strength, and hardness.

3.1.3.4 *Multiscale*

A product digital twin describes both the macroscopic characteristics (such as geometric dimensions) and microscopic characteristics (such as material microstructure, surface roughness, etc.) of the physical product.

3.1.3.5 *Hierarchical*

All the different components and parts that make up the final product can have their corresponding digital twins. For example, aircraft digital twins include digital twins for the airframe, flight control system, propulsion control system, etc. These are conducive to the hierarchical and refined management of product data and models and for the gradual realization of product digital twins.

3.1.3.6 Integrated

The product digital twin is a multiscale and multilevel integrated model of various aspects, such as the physical structure model, geometric model, and material. This is conducive to the rapid simulation and analysis of the overall structural and mechanical characteristics of the product.

3.1.3.7 Dynamic

Throughout the product lifecycle, the product digital twin constantly interacts with the product and is improved continuously. For example, collected product manufacturing data (such as inspection data and progress data) will be reflected in the digital twin to enable real-time, dynamic, and visual monitoring of the manufacturing status and process.

3.1.3.8 Hyper-realistic

The product digital twin is basically identical to the actual product in appearance, substance, and nature. Such realistic simulation accurately reflects the true state of the physical product.

3.1.3.9 Computable

The state and behavior of the corresponding physical entity can be simulated and reflected in real time through simulation, computation, and analysis of the product digital twin.

3.1.3.10 Probabilistic

Probability and statistics can be used to compute and simulate product digital twins.

3.1.3.11 Multidisciplinary

The product digital twin is multidisciplinary. It involves the intersection and fusion of multiple disciplines, such as computer science, information science, mechanical engineering, electronics, and physics.

3.1.4 The core position of the product digital twin

3.1.4.1 Product lifecycle and value chain data center

The product digital twin takes the product as the carrier. The product digital twin involves the entire product lifecycle, from conceptual design through detailed design, process design, manufacturing, and subsequent usage, maintenance, and scrapping/recycling.

On the one hand, the product digital twin is the data center of the product lifecycle, and its value is in providing a single data source and information continuity at all stages of the product lifecycle.

On the other hand, the product digital twin is the data center of the entire value chain, and its value is in information sharing and allowing seamless collaboration along the entire value chain. Examples include collaborative design and development among vendors from different time zones and regions, assembly simulation between upstream and downstream, and product testing and improvement through virtual usage.

3.1.4.2 Expansion and extension of PLM

PLM focuses on the management of products through their BOMs, such as the design BOM, process BOM, manufacturing BOM, and sales BOM.

The product digital twin not only emphasizes the linkage of information from all stages of the product lifecycle using a single product model, but also provides a single data source for product development, manufacturing, usage and maintenance, engineering changes, and vendor collaboration.

In addition, the product digital twin associates all aspects of product manufacturing and service data with the product model, so that companies can use the data more efficiently to optimize and improve product design and use the product digital twin to predict and control the formation process and status of product entities in reality, thereby realizing unified management and effective usage of data from the entire value chain. Therefore, the product digital twin can be said to be an extension of PLM.

3.1.4.3 Evolution and expansion of product design for manufacture and assembly

Conventionally, Design for Manufacture and Assembly (DFMA) combines design and process integration so that the various requirements and constraints of the manufacturing process (including capacity, accuracy, capability, etc.) are taken into consideration in the design modeling process. Using effective modeling and analysis, the convenience and economy of both design outcomes and manufacturing are ensured. Similarly, the product digital twin supports the evaluation of product manufacturability through modeling, simulation, and optimization at the product design stage. At the same time, it supports product performance and function testing as well as verification. Historical data, manufacturing data, usage and maintenance data, etc., are also used to optimize and improve product design. One of its goals is product design over the entire product lifecycle, which is an evolution and expansion of DFMA.

3.1.4.4 *The next iteration of product modeling, simulation, and optimization technology*

Over the past few decades, simulation technology has been primarily used as a computing tool by engineers to solve specific design and engineering problems. In its Defense Manufacturing in 2010 and Beyond plan, the United States listed design tools based on modeling and simulation as one of the four core capabilities to prioritize. In recent years, with the emergence and development of model-based system engineering (MBSE), new ground has been broken in product modeling and simulation with the central concept of "communication through simulation." Currently, simulation technology is still considered a product development tool.

With the emergence and development of product digital twins, simulation technology will become a core product/system function in subsequent lifecycle stages (such as completion of delivery before the physical products, simulation-driven assisted product usage support, etc.). The product digital twin facilitates the seamless integration of modeling, simulation, and optimization technologies into all stages of the product lifecycle (such as supporting product usage and services through direct association with product usage data), marking the next step in the development of such technologies.

3.1.4.5 *Emphasis on virtual control and the integration of virtual and real*

The basic function of the product digital twin is to reflect/mirror the real state and behavior of the corresponding product entity for virtual control and the integration of virtual and real. On the one hand, the product digital twin uses actual data to improve and integrate its records and construct models; on the other hand, it monitors and controls the physical product and its surroundings in real time by displaying, analyzing, processing, and performing statistical calculations on such data.

It is worth noting that deep integration of virtual and real is the prerequisite for realizing virtual control. Product manufacturing is based on the product model definition in virtual space, and both the continued evolution of the product model in virtual space and the generation of decisions are based on data collected in reality.

3.2   Digital Twin and PLM

3.2.1   Digital twin architecture

At present, there are relatively few systematic research outcomes for product digital twin worldwide. The following is a proposal for a product digital twin architecture, as shown in Figure 3-3, based on an analysis of the data composition, implementation, function, and aim of product digital twin from the perspective of the product lifecycle.

3.2.2   The manifestation of digital twin at each stage of the lifecycle

3.2.2.1   Product design stage

In the product design phase, using digital twins can improve design accuracy and verify real-life product performance. At this stage, the digital twin mainly has the following two functions:

1) Digital model design. Build a fully-annotated 3D product model that includes "3D design model + Product Manufacturing Information (PMI) + other relevant attributes." Specifically, the PMI includes the geometric dimensions and tolerances of the physical product, as well as 3D annotations, surface roughness, surface treatment methods, welding symbols, technical requirements, process notes, material schedules, etc. "Other relevant attributes" include part number, coordinate system, material, version, date, etc.

2) Simulation. Use a series of simulations that are repeatable, have variable parameters, and can be accelerated to verify product performance in different external environments to verify the product's adaptability during the design phase.

   For example, in the automotive design process, due to energy-saving and emission-reduction requirements, Dassault used its CAD and CAE platform, 3Dexperience, to help auto makers, including BMW, Tesla, and Toyota accurately perform aerodynamics and fluid acoustics analysis and simulation. As for exterior design, the use of data analysis and simulation has greatly improved aerodynamics to reduce air resistance (Figure 3-4).

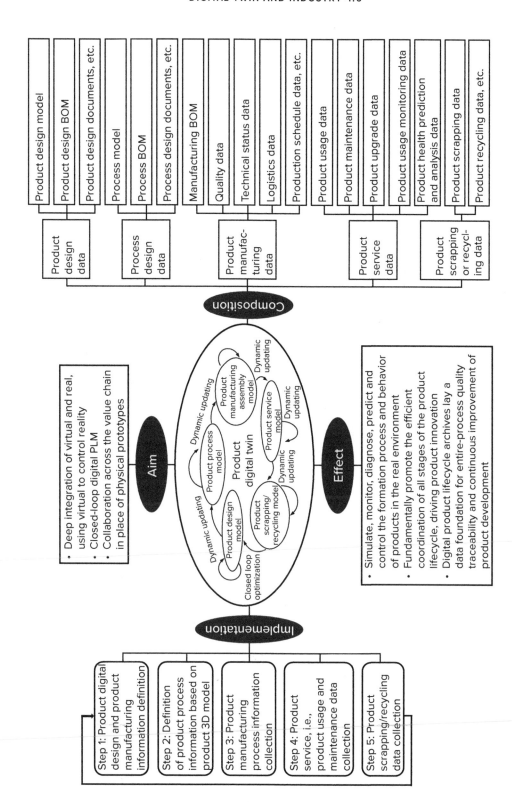

Figure 3-3 Schematic of the product digital twin architecture

Physical asset

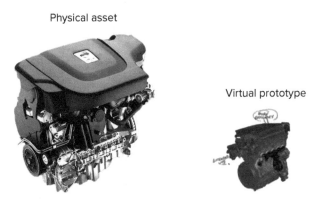

Virtual prototype

Figure 3-4 Application of digital twin in the product design phase

3.2.2.2 Process design stage

On the basis of "3D design model + PMI + other relevant attributes," process design based on the 3D product model is realized. The specific implementation steps include 3D design model conversion, 3D process modeling, structured process design, 3D model-based tooling design, 3D process simulation verification, and the establishment of a standards library. Finally, Model Based Instructions (MBI) are formed based on digital models and include process BOM, 3D process simulation animation, and associated process text information and documents.[15]

3.2.2.3 Manufacturing stage

The main implementation during the manufacturing stage includes the Product Memory and the Product Data Package, that is, the collection of manufacturing information and full-factor reconstruction, including Manufacture BOM (MBOM), quality data, technical status data, logistics data, product inspection data, production schedule data, reverse process data, etc. The three main functions are shown in Table 3-3.

Table 3-3   The three functions of digital twin at the manufacturing stage

1	Manufacturing process simulation
2	Digital production line
3	Key indicators monitoring and process capability assessment

1) Production process simulation. Prior to production, virtual production can be used to simulate the production process with different products, parameters, and external conditions, so as to predict production capacity, efficiency, and possible bottlenecks. This would accelerate the introduction of new products and make the process more accurate.

2) Digital production line. Various elements of the manufacturing stage, such as raw materials, equipment, process formulae, and process requirements, are integrated into a closely-coordinated production process through digital means, and operations with different combinations of conditions are automatically completed according to established rules to achieve automated production processes. At the same time, various data in the production process are recorded to provide a reliable basis for subsequent analysis and optimization.

3) Key-indicator monitoring and process capability evaluation. Through the collection of real-time operating data from various equipment of the production line, visual monitoring of the entire production process is achieved, and monitoring strategies for key equipment parameters and inspection indicators are established through experience or machine learning, so that anomalies are dealt with in time for a stable and continuously-optimized production process.

   For example, the online quality-monitoring system built for a cover glass production line collects the data generated by equipment at both the cold and hot ends before using machine learning to obtain the best specifications of the key indicators in the production process. The corresponding SPC monitoring alarm strategy is set, and through correlation analysis, the diagnosis and analysis of anomalies of specific qualities are carried out at tens of thousands of data collection points.

3.2.2.4 Product service stage

As IoT technology matures and sensors become cheaper, many industrial products (from capital equipment to consumer-grade items) use a large number of sensors to collect data about the operating environment and operational status when the product is being operated. Data analysis and optimization are then used to minimize or even prevent malfunctions to improve the user experience. In this stage, the digital twin has three functions (Table 3-4).

Table 3-4   The three functions of digital twin in the product service stage

1	Remote monitoring and predictive maintenance
2	Optimize customers' production indicators
3	Product usage feedback

1) Remote monitoring and predictive maintenance. By obtaining various parameters of the sensors or control systems for intelligent industrial products in real time, visual remote monitoring is established. Using the historical data collected, a health indicator system for the hierarchical components, subsystems, and even the entire equipment is constructed, and AI is then used to predict trends.

Based on those predictions, maintenance and the management of spare parts are optimized to reduce and avoid losses and conflicts that customers suffer due to unplanned downtime.

2) Optimize customers' production indicators. For customers who rely on industrial equipment for production, the rationality of industrial equipment parameter settings and the adaptability of such equipment under different production conditions determine their product quality and delivery cycle time.

Industrial equipment manufacturers can build empirical models for different application scenarios and production processes by collecting large amounts of data. This would help their customers optimize parameter configuration and improve product quality and production efficiency.

3) Product usage feedback. By collecting real-time operating data from intelligent industrial products, industrial equipment manufacturers can gain insights into the real needs of their customers. By doing so, they can help their customers shorten the introduction stage of new products, avoid malfunctions caused by product misuse, and improve the accuracy of product parameter configurations. Additionally, it allows them to better grasp customer needs, thereby avoiding mistakes in R&D decisions.

For example, the predictive maintenance and fault auxiliary diagnosis system developed by NeuCloud for oil drilling equipment collects in real time the various key indicators from different subsystems of the drilling rig, such as generators, mud pumps, winches, and top drives. Based on the trends in the historical data, the system then evaluates the performance of key components and adjusts and optimizes maintenance strategies based on component performance predictions. At the same time, it can also evaluate and optimize the drilling rig's efficiency by analyzing its status in real time, effectively raising the input-output ratio of drilling. Figure 3-5 shows the application of digital twin in the product service stage.

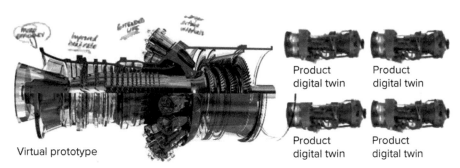

Figure 3-5 Application of digital twin in the product usage stage

3.2.2.5 Product scrapping/recycling stage

In this stage, product scrapping/recycling data is recorded, including the reasons for scrapping/recycling, dates, actual product life, etc. After the product is scrapped/recycled, all models and data in its digital twin will become part of the historical data of the same product type and be archived. The archived data is used for improving the design and innovation of future products, for quality analysis and predictions for the same type of product, and for optimizing the simulation and analysis models based on physical products.

Combining the above five stages, the implementation of product digital twin is observed to have the three characteristics, as shown in Table 3-5.

Table 3-5   The three characteristics of product digital twin implementation

1	It caters to the entire product lifecycle, and a single data source is used to achieve a two-way connection between physical space and information space.
2	The product archives must ensure all parts are traceable (such as actual materials). They must also ensure the traceability of quality data (such as dimensions, processing/assembly errors, and deformations) and technical status (such as technical indicators and the actual manufacturing process).
3	In the service stage, after the product is manufactured, two-way connection and communication with the physical product is still needed for product monitoring, tracking, behavior prediction and control, health prediction and management, etc., for closed-loop product lifecycle data management.

3.2.3 Digital twin implementation at each stage in the product lifecycle

3.2.3.1 Product design stage

As a hyper-realistic dynamic model of a physical product in virtual space, a product digital twin first requires a digital means of expression that is easy to understand, accurate, efficient, and supports data definitions and transmission of all stages in the product lifecycle, such as product design, process design, processing, assembly, usage, maintenance, etc.

Model-based definition (MBD) has emerged in recent years is an effective way to solve this problem, becoming one of the important means to realize product digital twins.

MBD is a methodology that uses 3D solid models and their associated data to define products. The aggregation of this data is also called a 3D digital data set which includes overall dimensions, geometric dimensions and tolerances, component materials, features and geometric relationships, contours, design intents, BOM, and other details. MBD enables product definition data to drive the various downstream segments of the manufacturing process, fully embodying the concept of parallel and collaborative product design and single data-source thinking, which is at the core of digital twin. The content structure of the MBD model is shown in Figure 3-6.

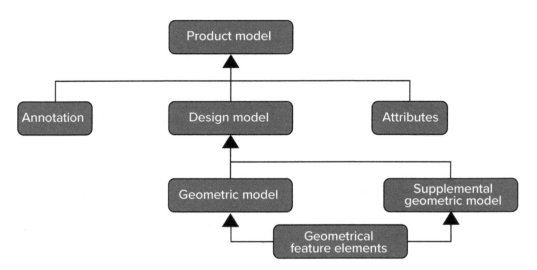

Figure 3-6 Content structure of the **MBD** model

The MBD model mainly includes the following two types of data: first, geometric information i.e., the product design model; and second, non-geometric information stored in the specification tree, responsible for storing and managing the data together with the PDM software supporting the 3D design software.

Finally, after coming up with the product definition based on the 3D model, it is necessary to simulate and optimize process design, tooling design, the manufacturing process, and even the process of product testing and verification based on the MBD model.

The three factors needed to ensure the accuracy of simulation and optimization outcomes are shown in Table 3-6.

Table 3-6   The three factors needed to ensure the accuracy of simulation and optimization results

1	Highly accurate/hyper-realistic virtual product model
2	Real-time and accurate simulation
3	Lightweight model technology

1) Highly accurate/hyper-realistic virtual product model. The modeling of products has to go beyond geometric features (such as shape, size, and tolerance) to include physical characteristics (such as stress analysis, dynamics, thermodynamics, material stiffness, plasticity, flexibility, elasticity, fatigue strength, etc.). Through the use of AI, machine learning, etc., historical data of similar groups of products can be used for the continuous optimization of existing models so that the virtual product models approximate the functions and characteristics of the physical products.

2) Real-time and accurate simulation. Advanced simulation platforms and software can be used, such as Ansys and Abaqus.

3) Lightweight model technology. This is a key technology for realizing product digital twin.

First, it greatly reduces the storage size of the model, so that the geometric, feature, and attribute information required for product process design and simulation can be directly extracted from the 3D model(s), reducing information redundancy.

Second, lightweight model technology makes possible product simulation visualization, complex system simulation, production line simulation, and product simulation based on real-time data.

Finally, the lightweight model speeds up information transmission between systems, reducing time and costs. It promotes the "end-to-end" integration of the value chain, information-sharing between upstream and downstream enterprises in the supply chain, business process integration, and collaborative product design and development.

3.2.3.2 Product manufacturing stage

The evolution and improvement of product digital twins are carried out through continuous interaction with product entities.

During the manufacturing stage, actual production data (such as inspection, progress, and logistics data) is transmitted to the virtual product and displayed in real time. This enables the monitoring of both manufacturing data measured in real time as well as the manufacturing process (including the comparison of design and measured value(s), the comparison of actual and design material characteristics, the comparison of planned and actual completion, etc.) based on the product model. In addition, the prediction and analysis of quality, manufacturing resources, and production schedule are realized, based on actual production data and the intelligent prediction and analysis of logistics and scheduling. The intelligent decision-making module formulates corresponding solutions based on the prediction and analysis outcomes before feeding back to the actual products, so as to achieve dynamic control over and optimization of physical products. This fusion of virtual and real enables the virtual control of reality.

Therefore, how to achieve the real-time and accurate collection of multi-source heterogeneous data in a complex and dynamic physical space, the effective extraction, and reliable transmission of information, are prerequisites for the realization of product digital twins. In recent years, the rapid development of technologies such as the IoT, sensor networks, Industrial Internet, semantic analysis, and recognition has provided a set of practical solutions to this end. In addition, the rapid development of AI, machine learning, data mining, high-performance computing, and other technologies provides important technical support. Figure 3-7 takes the assembly process as an example of establishing a digital twin implementation framework for manufacturing processes. As the assembly line is the carrier of product assembly, the framework considers both the product and the assembly line digital twins.

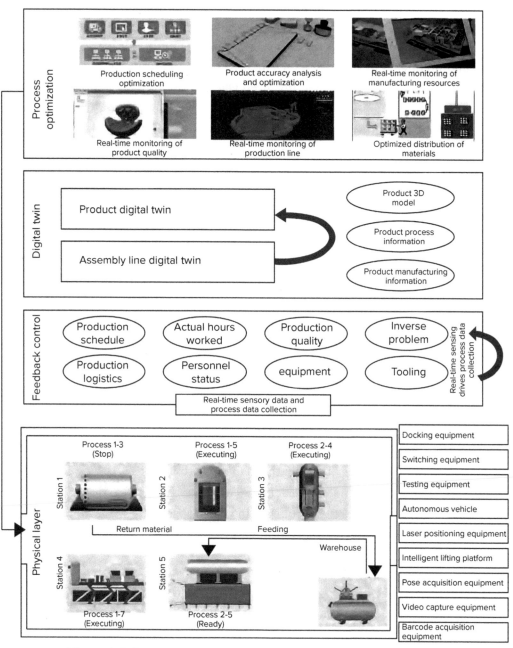

Figure 3-7 Schematic of a digital twin implementation framework for manufacturing processes

3.2.3.3 *Product service stage*

At this stage, it is still necessary to track and monitor the product status in real time, including its physical location, external environment, quality, usage, technical and functional status, etc. Based on the product's actual condition, real-time data, and usage and maintenance records, its health, lifespan, functions, and performance are forecasted and analyzed to provide advanced warning of product quality problems. At the same time, when a product malfunctions or when quality issues surface, it can be quickly located, the fault and quality issue(s) recorded and cause(s) analyzed, the parts replaced, and the product serviced, upgraded, scraped, or even decommissioned.

On the one hand, the IoT, sensor technology, and mobile Internet are used to map measured data from the product (such as the latest sensor, location, external environment data, etc.), usage and maintenance data, etc., onto the product digital twin. On the other hand, in the virtual space, model visualization technology is used for the real-time monitoring of product usage. Together with historical usage and maintenance data, as well as relevant historical data from the same product type, Bayesian methods and machine learning are used for data mining and optimization. Through this, prediction and analysis models for the product, structural analysis, thermodynamics, and product failure and lifespan are continuously optimized to make the product digital twin and predictive analysis models more accurate and simulation prediction outcomes more in line with reality.

For physical products that have failed or displayed quality issues, tracing and simulation technologies are used to quickly locate the product, analyze causes, generate solutions, verify feasibility, etc., with the outcomes fed back to the physical world for troubleshooting and tracing. Just as in the manufacturing process, the implementation framework of digital twins in the product service process mainly includes data collection in the physical world, digital twin evolution in virtual space, and status monitoring and optimization control based on digital twins.[16]

3.3 The Interpretation of Digital Twin by Large Software Companies

With the continuous development of AI, VR, and the IoT, digital twins are being widely applied in manufacturing. According to the International Data Corporation (IDC), 40% of large software companies now use virtual simulation to model production processes, and digital twin is an Industry 4.0 solution for manufacturers.

Since the birth of the digital twin concept, how to correctly translate the term has become the focus of the industry. Various major software companies have put forth their interpretations of digital twin and integrated them into their businesses to create solutions that bridge the real and virtual worlds.

3.3.1 Siemens

In 2016, Siemens acquired CD-adapco, a global engineering simulation software supplier that provides software solutions across a range of engineering disciplines such as Computational Fluid Dynamics (CFD), Compatibility Support Module (CSM), heat transfer, particle dynamics, feed flow, electrochemistry, acoustics, and rheology.

Siemens has a unique understanding of the digital twin concept:

1) Dr. Qi Feng, General Manager of Siemens Industry Software for Greater China DER, says: "The aims of digital twin are to discover potential problems, stimulate innovative thinking, and achieve continuous optimization and improvement. There are two necessary conditions for realizing digital twins, namely a set of integrated software tools and 3D representation."

2) Dr. Jan Mrosik, CEO of the Siemens Digital Factory Division, says that digital twins simulate the actual operating space (such as the production lines) in some factories to a high degree of accuracy. "They can tell us clearly whether the final systems are able to withstand various conditions to achieve success."

3) Mr. Liang Naiming, Senior Global Vice President of the Siemens Digital Factory Division and Managing Director for Greater China, believes that in the final analysis, transforming the manufacturing industry entails going back to the basics, i.e., ensuring speed, flexibility, efficiency, quality, and safety. The key to achieving all these is to integrate both the physical and virtual worlds using digital twin. Siemens's digital twin entails product to production design, OEM mechanical design, factory planning and scheduling, manufacturing, and using final product Big Data to monitor products, factories, factory clouds, and product clouds.

CD-adapco software coupled with Simcenter, Siemens multidisciplinary simulation product, combines simulation and physical testing, intelligent reporting, and data analysis technology to better assist customers in creating digital twins and more accurately predicting product performance at various stages of product development.

Siemens's comprehensive simulation software and testing solutions not only support its digitalization strategy and system-driven product development, but also promote innovation at all stages of product development, laying a solid foundation for its digital twin strategy.

3.3.2 GE

On November 16, 2016, GE announced that it was partnering with Ansys to work on model-based digital twin technology. Through the cooperation, Ansys will work with GE's digital department, global research department, and industry department to expand and integrate Ansys's physical engineering simulation and embedded software R&D platform with GE's Predix Platform, so as to make use of digital twin solutions in different industries.

Extending digital twin solutions from the edge to the cloud will not only more quickly unlock the value of Ansys's simulation capability, but also promote the Predix Platform and create new opportunities for exploring breakthrough business models and business relationships (Figure 3-8).

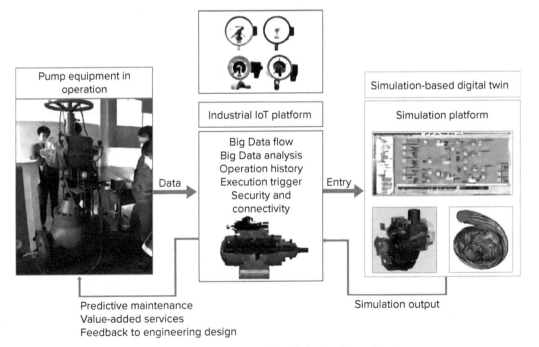

Figure 3-8 Schematic of GE's digital twin technology

For example, every engine, turbine, and nuclear magnetic resonance unit has a digital twin, and engineers can clearly see every detail of the machine's operation on a computer. Through these digital models, robots can be debugged, tested, and optimized in a virtual environment. Subsequently, the best solutions are used on physical machines, greatly lowering maintenance and debugging costs. After applying digital twin technology to the GE90 engines, the number of overhauls was reduced, saving tens of millions of dollars; after applying the digital twin technology to the railway, fuel efficiency was greatly improved, and emissions were reduced.

Marc-Thomas Schmidt, Chief Architect of the Predix Platform at GE Digital, points out, "One of the most exciting aspects of digital twins is that we can now look at an individual product system—such as a wind turbine—and isolate just that one product. We're not talking about a general class of turbines, but that one turbine. We can study the weather patterns that affect it, the angle of its blades, its energy output, and optimize that one piece of machinery. If we do this across all our product systems in the field, imagine the impact on overall product performance. This clearly represents a revolution in product engineering."

The cooperation between GE and Ansys shows that simulation technology is no longer just a tool for engineers to design better products and reduce physical testing costs. By creating digital twins, the application of simulation technology is extended to various operational fields, to even include product health management, remote diagnosis, smart maintenance, shared services, and more.

For example, through the rich sensor data provided by increasingly intelligent industrial equipment and the powerful predictive function of simulation technology, companies can now analyze specific working conditions and predict failure points, thereby lowering production and maintenance optimization costs.[17]

3.3.3   PTC

PTC CEO Jim Heppelmann believes the extension of PLM to product usage and the next design cycle will result in a closed-loop product design system process capable of carrying out preventive maintenance. PTC views this as the key link in its "Smart Connected Products" concept. Every action taken by a smart product will be made known to the designer to realize real-time feedback and revolutionize optimization strategies.

PTC hopes to combine technology with solutions. By predicting changes and providing the toolbox required for commercial success, technology is combined with solutions to meet the digitalization needs of the manufacturing industry. Focusing on the development of smart, connected products and product service, global monitoring will help customers overcome various challenges and make them more competitive in the manufacturing industry. PTC is working on a series of solutions covering the entire product lifecycle, from initial product conceptualization to the usage of thousands of products in the field. In the end, the information collected will be utilized in the design and development phase of next-generation products.

3.3.4 Oracle

Oracle believes that digital twin is a very important concept. As the IoT gains traction amongst companies, digital twin will become an operating strategy.

Oracle is implementing digital twin in its IoT Cloud in the three ways shown in Table 3-7.

Table 3-7 The three ways in which Oracle is implementing digital twin in its IoT Cloud

1	Virtual Twin Device virtualization, beyond the simple observables and expectations of JSON files
2	Predictive Twin Problem solution by simulating the complexity of actual products using models built with various technologies
3	Twin Projections Projecting insights generated by the digital twin onto the user's back-end business applications, making the IoT an integral part of the user's business infrastructure

3.3.5 SAP

SAP's digital twin system is based on the SAP Leonardo platform. The creation of a complete digital twin allows real-time engineering and R&D.

In the product usage phase, the SAP digital twin system collects and analyzes equipment operational data to measure actual performance before comparing this with design targets, forming a closed-loop product development system. This is of great significance to digital R&D and product innovation.

SAP and Mitsubishi Robotics jointly launched closed-loop digital product management (Figure 3-9) to help companies with product innovation. Specifically, SAP has launched a module for product requirement definition which guides the corresponding product development and design tasks.

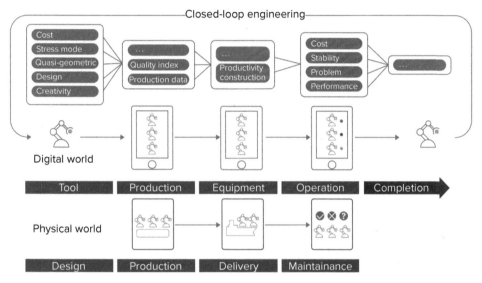

Figure 3-9 Closed-loop digital product management jointly launched by SAP and Mitsubishi Robotics

Cost analysis is then carried out using a cost estimation system based on in-memory calculation and Big Data analysis to guide product development. At the digital development stage, the mechanical, electrical, electronic, and design systems are integrated. Finally, the user accesses the SAP online ordering system to engage in real-time robot interactive design using a 3D interface.[18]

3.4 Development Trends in Digital Twin Manufacturing

3.4.1 Virtualization

The product digital twin is a true reflection of the physical product in virtual space. The successful industrial application of product digital twins depends on their fidelity, i.e., the degree of similitude. Each physical property of the product has its own specific model, including the CFD model, structural dynamics model, thermodynamic model, stress analysis model, fatigue damage model, and material state evolution model (the evolution of material stiffness, strength, fatigue strength, etc.). How to associate these models based on different physical attributes is the key to establishing a product digital twin for simulation, diagnosis, prediction, and control.

Simulation results based on the multiphysical integrated model can more accurately reflect and mirror the actual state and behavior of physical products, making it possible to do away with physical prototypes by instead testing product functions and performance virtually. In addition, this can resolve the problems of time and geometry, when forecasting the health and remaining lifespan of products, which arise from the use of conventional methods (analyzing the model corresponding to each physical characteristic separately and not jointly). For instance, the US AFRL built a digital twin that integrates different physical attributes to accurately predict aircraft lifespan. Therefore, multiphysical modeling will provide an important technical means to improve the simulation of product digital twins so they can perform their roles more fully.

3.4.2 Encompassing the entire lifecycle

At this stage, research on product digital twin mainly focuses on the stages of product design or after-sales service and rarely involves product manufacturing.

NASA and the AFRL have built product digital twins to accurately predict potential quality problems during product usage/service, so products can be accurately located and quickly traced when quality issues arise.

In the future, research and applications involving product digital twins at the manufacturing stage will become a hot topic. For example, manufacturing process data is associated with the corresponding "unit model" and "unit information-processing model" in the product digital twin, realizing association mapping between virtual and physical products. The resulting 3D model can be displayed on a screen and can also interact with the physical product in multiple dimensions, such as highlighting anomalies that require attention, automatically comparing measured and design data, and automatically verifying/analyzing the feasibility of subsequent operations.

This real-time interaction between virtual and physical products will increase efficiency and improve quality in the manufacturing stage. Taking the precision analysis of a seeker optical system as an example, during production the collected inspection data is transmitted to the product digital twin in real time so both actual and theoretical design data can be displayed and intuitively compared. On the other hand, actual measurement data is used to calculate and analyze both processing and assembly errors. The amount of process compensation can be determined using the process parameter calculation module in the product digital twin. Based on the stability and consistency of the system, real-time compensation and control of both processing and assembly errors are carried out. Following this, the process compensation is used to determine the overall system compensation. This would drive the actuator to issue instructions for completing process compensation through assembly operations. By optimizing assembly parameters, existing measurement data can be used to predict the optical performance, anti-vibration, and thermal shock capabilities of the final optical system. Decisions can then be made based on the predictions.

Another example would be using the new generation of infocommunication technologies such as the IoT, Industrial Internet, and mobile Internet for the real-time collection and processing of process data (such as equipment operating data, production logistics data, production schedule data, production personnel data, etc.) before mapping and matching the data with product and production line digital twins. This would allow for refined online control of the manufacturing process (including control of the production progress, product technical status control, production site logistics control, product quality control, etc.).

Data mining techniques such as intelligent cloud platforms, and dynamic Bayesian and neural networks are then combined with machine learning algorithms to achieve the real-time dynamic optimization and adjustment of production lines, manufacturing modules, production schedules, logistics, and quality.

3.4.3   Integration

As the enabling technology of product digital twins, digital thread technology is used to realize the two-way interaction between models and key data at each stage of the digital twin's lifecycle. It is the basis for realizing a single product data source and efficient collaboration at all stages of the product lifecycle. The US Department of Defense regards digital thread technology as the fundamental technology for digital manufacturing, and the Alliance of Industrial Internet also regards it as a key technology to address. At present, product design, process design, manufacturing, inspection, and usage are still disjointed segments, and the continuous flow of digital data has not been fully realized.

Although the emergence of MBD technology has enhanced and standardized the description of manufacturing information based on 3D product models, this is mainly confined to the product and process design stages and needs to be extended to the manufacturing/assembly, inspection, and usage stages. Moreover, current digital flow is one-way, and digital thread technology is needed to enable the two-way flow. Therefore, the integration of digital thread and digital twin is a future development trend.

3.4.4 Integration with AR technology

In AR technology, the position and angle of the camera image are calculated in real time before corresponding images are added. The goal of the technology is to overlay the virtual world on the physical world on a screen for interaction. In product design and manufacturing, AR technology is introduced to integrate a 3D immersive virtual platform with reality. Through virtual peripherals, what developers and production personnel see and perceive in virtual reality is synchronized with the physical world, and manipulating the virtual model affects the physical world. This has applications in product design, formulation of technical processes, and control of production processes. AR technology demolishes the boundary between us and virtual reality by enhancing what we see, hear, and touch. This blurs the boundary and further integrates our world with virtual reality as we are no longer confined to the 2D worlds on our screens. Instead, we can experience and influence the physical world through virtual reality. The integration of AR technology and product digital twin will be one of the important directions in the development of digital design and manufacturing technology, modeling and simulation technology, and VR technology. It is the fusion of the real and the virtual at a higher level.[19]

CHAPTER 4

DIGITAL TWIN CITY

" Digital twin city" is the broad application of digital twin technology at the city level. By building a complex and massive system that maps the physical city to virtual reality and enables collaborative interaction, an online twin is created in which all elements of the city are digitalized and virtualized. The city's state is displayed in real-time and can be visualized, with city management decision-making now coordinated and smarter.

To sum up, the essence of digital twin city is the mapping of physical cities in virtual space. It is also a complex and comprehensive technological system that supports the building of smart cities. This coexistence of physical and virtual cities, and the fusion of the real and the virtual, is the future of urban development.

4.1 The Rise of the Digital Twin City Concept

There are many existing problems with urban development, and the shortcomings of the conventional development model are increasingly obvious. Digital and smart cities that are powered by informatization are new urban development concepts and models. China, for example, has seen three waves of smart city construction (Figure 4-1).[20]

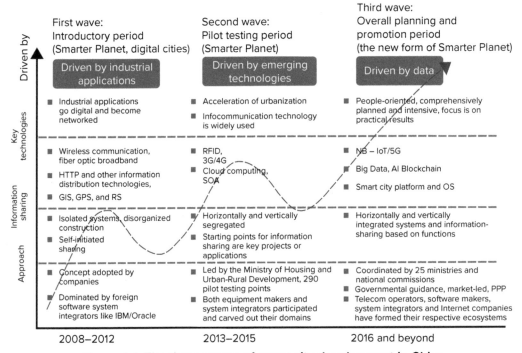

Figure 4-1 The three waves of smart city development in China

4.1.1 2008–2012: Introductory period

This marked the first wave of smart cities in China, which was driven by industrial applications. Key technologies included wireless communication, fiber optic broadband, HTTP, GIS, and GPS technologies. Information systems tended to be department-or system-based and were constructed individually, leading to many isolated islands of information, while most information sharing was spontaneous and "point-to-point." The development of the smart city industry was also dominated by foreign software system integrators who introduced the concept.

4.1.2   2013–2015: Pilot testing period

The second wave started as these smart cities developed Chinese characteristics. Against the backdrop of accelerating urbanization in China, this period focuses on the comprehensive application of RFID, 3G/4G, cloud computing, SOA, and other information technologies. System building became horizontally and vertically segmented, and information sharing revolved around exchange platforms, with key projects or collaborative applications as the starting points. The Ministry of Housing and Urban-Rural Development took the lead in promoting the initiative and selected 290 locations nationwide for pilot testing to fully explore the path and mode of smart city building. Both foreign and domestic software makers, system integrators, and equipment vendors actively participated.

4.1.3   2016 and beyond: Overall planning and promotion period

In 2016, the Chinese government rolled out a new smart city concept that is data-driven, people-oriented, comprehensively planned, and intensive, focusing on practical results. Key technologies include NB-IoT, 5G, Big Data, AI, blockchain, smart city platforms, and operating systems, etc. Information systems evolved in the direction of horizontally and vertically integrated large systems, and information-sharing became based on functions instead of campaigns. Promotion efforts are now coordinated by 25 ministries and national commissions. In the market, telecom operators, software makers, system integrators, and Internet companies have formed their respective ecosystems and settled into a market-led situation with government guidance.

Although the digital city concept has been around for a long time, it did not reach the heights of digital twin due to technological constraints. Today, the connotation of digital twin city truly reflects the vision and goals that digital cities seek to achieve. The smart city is an advanced stage of urban development. As the goal of urban development, the digital twin city is the new starting point for building a smart city. It provides important facilities and core capabilities for the realization of smart cities. It marks the transformation of technologically-driven urban informatization from quantity to quality and from point to line and line to surface. Based on advanced technological capabilities such as digital identification, automatic sensing, networked connections, intelligent control, and platform services, the digital city model has taken shape. As a twin, it runs in parallel with the physical city, fusing virtual and real, and contains endless possibilities for innovation.

Digital twin cities have the characteristic of precise mapping, which means they can achieve comprehensive digital modeling of urban infrastructure, such as roads, bridges, manhole covers, lampposts, and buildings by deploying sensors at various levels, including the air, ground, underground, and waterways. They also enable full perception and dynamic monitoring of the city's operational status, forming an accurate information expression and mapping of the physical city in the information dimension of the virtual city. In addition, traces are left behind in constructing urban infrastructure and various components, and information is available when city residents and visitors connect to the Internet. In the future digital twin cities, various traces can be observed in the physical urban space, and various information can be searched in the virtual urban space. Urban planning, construction, and the population's activities are greatly expanded in the physical and virtual spaces. The integration of the virtual and the real, as well as the coordination between them, will define a new model for the future development of cities.

Designing digital twin cities will ultimately empower comprehensive urban management from multiple perspectives. Digital twin integrates various new information technologies, breaks down technological silos with a platform-based approach, and endows cities with functions, such as holistic perception, information interaction, and precise control, thereby improving the overall operational level of cities.

Therefore, digital twin technology can be fully utilized for the third wave of smart city development in China. Dynamic monitoring based on 3D sensing, timely response based on ubiquitous networks, real-time analysis based on software models, and scientific decision-making using urban brain solutions can be utilized to tackle the complexities and uncertainties in the closed-loop process of urban design, building, management, and service. This will comprehensively improve the allocation efficiency and operational condition(s) of urban material resources, intellectual resources, and information resources, generating endogenous momentum for smart city development.

4.2　The Four Characteristics of Digital Twin City

Digital twin city has the four characteristics shown in Table 4-1.

Table 4-1　The four characteristics of digital twin city

1	Accurate mapping
2	Interaction between virtual and real
3	Software defined
4	Smart intervention

4.2.1　Accurate mapping

Comprehensive digital modeling of roads, bridges, manhole covers, lamp covers, buildings, and other infrastructure is achieved through the deployment of sensors in the air, on the ground, underground, in rivers, etc. At the same time, comprehensive sensing and dynamic monitoring of the city's operating status enables the physical city to be accurately expressed and mapped onto the virtual twin.

4.2.2　Interaction between virtual and real

The construction of urban infrastructure and facilities will leave traces that residents and visitors can obtain more information about online. In digital twin cities, such traces would be observable in the physical city, while various kinds of information can be found online in the virtual twin. Urban planning, facilities, and resident activities will no longer be restricted to the physical world. This fusion and collaboration of virtual and real will define a new model of urban development.

4.2.3　Software defined

The digital twin city is a virtual model that corresponds to the physical city and simulates the behavior of people, events, and things using software.

Cloud and edge computing are used to control the city's traffic signals, manage power supplies and major projects, and aid site-choosing and construction of infrastructure.

4.2.4 Smart intervention

By using the digital twin city for planning, design, and simulation, early warnings can be intelligently provided for possible adverse effects, conflicts, and potential risks. At the same time, reasonable and feasible countermeasures would be suggested. This smart intervention in the city's original development trajectory and operation through a future-oriented perspective will then guide and optimize the planning and management of physical cities, improving the delivery of services to residents and making urban living smarter. In particular, artificial intelligence is merely a means of implementation in the governance of smart cities, while the core lies in constructing the digital twin city.[21]

4.3 Digital Twin City Service Form(s) and Typical Scenario(s)

4.3.1 Service form(s)

4.3.1.1 Scenario

All urban service scenarios will be mapped onto virtual scenarios online. 3D visualization means are then used to present both the static and dynamic service scenario information in the city brain (Table 4-2).

Table 4-2 Digital twin city service scenarios

1	Static information Including geospatial information such as location and area, building information such as floors and rooms, pipeline information such as water, electricity, and heating, and equipment information such as elevators
2	Dynamic information Including environmental information such as temperature and humidity, energy consumption information, equipment operation information, people flow information, etc.

In addition, service scenarios can be static, such as at government service points, museums, libraries, hospitals, nursing homes, schools, stadiums, shopping centers, and community service centers, or dynamic, such as on buses and subways. Activities such as government services, sporting events and concerts, borrowing books from a library, visiting a museum, shopping, attending lessons, etc., can now be completed online through technologies such as digital twin and VR. Such a change reduces transport, time, and financial costs while the experience is not compromised. Digital twin services are different from conventional online services because the setting, business processes, service efficiency, etc., can be fully replicated and even surpass reality.

4.3.1.2 Target

Urban services are people-oriented. Currently, the more commonly encountered user profiles are limited to a few basic tags and some behavioral attributes. This is the nascent form of digital twin. Building on user profiles, digital twin will integrate basic personal information, monitoring information covering the entire area, ubiquitous sensing information, all-encompassing service organization information, mobile phone signals, online behavior, etc., so that everyone is tracked around the clock. By doing so, every person's tracks, expressions, actions, and social ties are simultaneously captured by his or her digital twin in real time. In the future, everyone will be accompanied by a digital twin from cradle to grave. The digital twin will contain an exact copy of the information on the person's physical state, movement, behavioral characteristics, etc.

4.3.1.3 Content

With the rapid development of technologies such as AR and VR, digital twins for urban services may be the first to be realized. VR provides an immersive experience through audio and video content. In the future, people will be able to enjoy immersive experiences without going to concerts or sports games in person. AR seamlessly integrates virtual information with the physical environment to provide virtual information services such as automotive head-up displays, guided museum tours, clinical assistance, etc.

4.3.2 Typical scenarios

Four typical digital twin city scenarios are shown in Table 4-3.

Table 4-3   Four typical scenarios of digital twin city

1	Intelligent planning and scientific evaluation
2	Urban management and social governance
3	Human-machine interaction in public services
4	Collaborative management and control scenarios throughout the entire lifecycle of a city

4.3.2.1 Intelligent planning and scientific evaluation

By using the digital twin city to analyze assumptions and carry out virtual planning, urban planning can be more targeted and done with greater foresight when the planners have details on the flora and fauna, roads and bridges and are in tune with how the city operates. Understanding the city's characteristics and evaluating the planning impact at the start of planning and construction help to avoid time wasted on impractical plans and designs and prevent the need for redesign during the verification stage. As such, the top-level design of a smart city, underpinned by innovative technologies, can be implemented using less time and money.

When it comes to evaluating the benefits of smart cities, using digital twin city and visualization, quantitative and qualitative methods are used to model and analyze urban traffic conditions, crowd distribution, air and water quality, etc., so that decision makers and evaluators can quickly and intuitively appreciate the improvements to the urban environment and city operations in smart cities. They can also evaluate the benefits of undertaking smart projects, utilizing urban data mining and analysis to assist the government in scientific decision-making for future informatization and smart-city building projects and avoid detours, repetition, and suboptimal efficiency.

4.3.2.2 Urban management and social governance

When building infrastructure, markers, sensors, communication and identification technologies—such as QR codes, RFID, 5G, etc.—can be used in urban facilities and infrastructure like underground pipe networks, multifunctional smart poles, charging points, smart manhole covers, smart trash cans, drones, cameras, etc. This allows the projects to be monitored, shared, modeled, and controlled to improve the maintenance of urban water supply, power supply, traffic systems, weather, ecosystems, and the overall environment.

For key scenarios such as urban traffic management, social governance, and emergency command, Big Data model simulations based on the digital twin can be used to perform precise data mining and scientific decision-making, dispatch commands and instructions, and monitor government decision-making to achieve dynamic, scientific, efficient, and safe urban management. Social incidents, urban components, and infrastructure will show up in the digital twin in real time, presented in multiple dimensions. For emergencies such as major public security incidents, fires, and floods, the digital twin can be used to identify the problem and relay orders in a matter of seconds. Thus, a single trigger is used to coordinate multiple parties to deploy in an orderly manner, with a reasonable division of the workload, and provide closed-loop feedback.

4.3.2.3 Human-machine interaction in public services

New smart city services revolve around residents, who are also a key consideration in urban planning and construction. With "people" as the core theme, the digital twin city will dynamically monitor and incorporate the daily trips, income levels, family structure, and daily expenditure of residents into models for coordinated computation. At the same time, "bit space" is used to predict population structure and migration patterns in order to plan where to locate future facilities, evaluate the impact of commercial projects, etc. Through intelligent human-machine interaction, reminders on websites, provision of smart services, etc., urban residents will be able to quickly access personalized government, education, cultural, health, and transportation services. The digital twin service system will wield much influence and have the power to reshape the urban space.

4.3.2.4 Collaborative management and control scenarios throughout the entire lifecycle of a city

By constructing an intelligent enabling system capable of sensing, evaluating, and responding quickly, collaborative innovation is made possible throughout the entire lifecycle of a city, such as during land surveying, planning, construction, operation, maintenance, etc.

Table 4-4 shows the collaborative management and control scenarios throughout the entire lifecycle of a city.

Table 4-4   The collaborative management and control scenarios throughout the entire lifecycle of a city

1	Surveying stage Based on numerical simulation, spatial analysis and visualization, a database of engineering survey information is built for the effective dissemination and sharing of engineering survey information.
2	Planning stage Connect with the smart urban spatiotemporal information service platform. Perform simulation analysis and visualization on the relevant plans and results to fully integrate multiple regulations.
3	Design stage Apply building information modeling and other technologies to perform functional and performance simulations, optimize, review, and deliver digital outcomes for the design schemes; carry out integrated collaborative design; and improve quality and efficiency.

(Continued)

97

4	Construction stage
	Use the information model to effectively supervise key processes such as schedule management, investment management, and labor management. Realize dynamic, integrated, and visual construction management.
5	Maintenance stage
	Utilize identification systems, sensing systems, and various intelligent facilities for the real-time monitoring, unified presentation, rapid response, and predictive maintenance of the city's overall system, improving operation and maintenance levels.

4.4 The Overall Architecture of Digital Twin City

Digital twin cities correspond to physical cities. To build a smart city, we need to build a digital twin for the city first. The digital twin concept did not exist previously, due to a lack of understanding and technical support. The rapid development of infocommunications technology means that the technical ability to build digital twin cities is now available: full-field 3D sensing, digitalized identification, the Internet of Trusted Things, ubiquitous computing for the masses, etc., all defined by intelligence and data-driven decision-making. Together this constitutes a powerful digital twin city technical model. New technologies and applications, such as Big Data, blockchain, AI, smart hardware, AR, VR, etc., improve the model and expand and enhance its functions. It is now possible to simulate and analyze problems that occur in the city.

Although the technical conditions are basically met, implementation is still quite complicated. This is not only a testing ground for the integration and innovation of new technologies but also a challenge to our wisdom.

The construction of a digital twin city relies on a technology ecosystem mainly composed of devices, networks, and the cloud, and its overall architecture is shown in Table 4-5.

Table 4-5   The overall digital twin city architecture

1	Device side | Full-field sensing of the city to closely reflect the physical status of its operation
2	Network side | Ubiquitous high-speed networks provide millisecond-level two-way data transmission, paving the way for intelligent interaction
3	Cloud side | Inclusive smart computing for large-scale, multiscale, long-term, and intelligent decision-making and intervention

4.4.1 Device side: crowdsensing, visible, controllable

Clusters of urban sensing devices provide crowdsensing capability. Sensing devices will rapidly develop from RFID and sensor nodes to smart hardware, poles, and unmanned vehicles with communication and computing capabilities. At the same time, smartphones and other personal terminals will have even more sophisticated sensing capabilities. With more powerful sensing, computing, storage, and communication capabilities, such devices will become powerful nodes for sensing the surrounding environment and residents of the city. This provides crowdsensing on a large scale using collaborative and pervasive computing.

Make conventional infrastructure smarter using intelligent signage and a sensing system. By building an integrated network of urban pipelines based on smart signs and monitoring, the coordination of planning, visualizations of construction and operations, and retention of all process data are made possible. Build a smart network of roads so that roads, barriers, bridges, etc., can be intelligently monitored, maintained, controlled, and managed. Multi-functional smart poles and other new smart equipment are fully deployed for smarter illumination, information exchange, wireless services, vehicle charging, emergency calls, environmental monitoring, and more.

4.4.2 Network side: ubiquitous, high-speed, one world

The network offers ubiquitous high-speed, multinetwork collaborative access services, enabling the comprehensive promotion of 4G/5G/WLAN/NB-IoT/eMTC and other multinetwork coordination. It achieves three-dimensional seamless coverage through virtualization and cloud technology, providing access services for wireless sensors, mobile broadband, and the Internet of Everything. Moreover, it supports next-generation converged applications for mobile communication networks in vertical industries.

A comprehensive "earth and space integration" information network is formed to support cloud services. Comprehensive utilization of new information network technology gives full play to the respective advantages of space-based, air-based, and land-based information technology: the effective acquisition, coordination, transmission, and aggregation of space-based, air-based, land-based, sea-based, and other multidimensional information. Beyond this, the overall planning and processing of resources, the distribution of tasks, and the organization and management of actions allow for the integrated and comprehensive processing of time-space complex networks. This, in turn, maximizes effective utilization, provide various users with a real-time, reliable, on-demand ubiquitous, mobile, efficient, intelligent, and collaborative information infrastructure and decision support system.

4.4.3 Cloud side: on-demand universal services benefitting residents

High-speed information processing is provided by edge and quantum computing facilities. Build edge computing nodes with surrounding sensing capability to distribute based on demand and provide intelligent feedback response in urban factories, roads, junction boxes, etc. Deploy various quantum computing equipment based on atoms, ions, superconducting circuits, and photons to support massive information processing tasks such as ultra-large-scale data retrieval, precise urban weather forecasting, computationally optimized traffic control, AI research, etc.

Utilize AI and blockchain for smart contracts. Build AI computing platforms that support knowledge inference, probabilistic statistics, deep learning, etc., and intelligent support capabilities for knowledge computing, cognitive inference, execution, and human-computer interaction. Construct customizable blockchain service facilities that support smart contracts by providing identity verification, electronic evidence preservation, supply chain management, and product traceability.

Deploy cloud computing and Big Data facilities. Build virtual integrated cloud computing service platforms, and Big Data analysis centers that allocate cross-regional server, network, and storage resources based on software-defined networking (SDN) technology to satisfy the storage and computing demands of smart government and public services, comprehensive governance, industrial development, etc.

The construction of digital twin cities will trigger disruptive innovations in intelligent urban management and services. A digital twin city contains the virtual image of every person, object, incident, building, road, facility, etc., in the physical city to enable information visualization, traceability, and status updates. The synchronization of the virtual with reality results in a blending of both; the past becomes traceable, and the future can be forecasted and extrapolated. Everything within the city is controllable, like a game of chess. Management becomes flatter, one-stop service becomes the norm, information becomes more accessible, and the public does not have to run around as much for government services. The virtual serves reality, and decision-making is based on simulation outcomes. As management becomes more refined and services become more personalized, smart cities are no longer just empty talk.[22]

CHAPTER 5

OTHER DIGITAL TWIN APPLICATIONS

5.1 Healthcare

By creating a digital twin of a hospital, hospital administrators, doctors, and nurses can be updated about patient health in real time (Figure 5-1). The digital twin for hospital healthcare management utilizes sensors to monitor patients, including wearable devices on their bodies. It coordinates the devices and personnel, providing a better way to analyze processes and alert relevant staff members at the right time for immediate action.

Hospital digital twins can improve the utilization of emergency rooms and better manage patient traffic to reduce operating costs and enhance the patient experience. In addition, digital twins can be used to predict and prevent patient emergencies based on a patient's heartbeat or breathing, thereby saving more lives. In fact, after a hospital implemented digital twin technology, it managed to reduce overall costs by 90% and blue code (emergency) incidents by 61%.

In the future, each of us will have our own digital twin. Through a variety of new medical tests, scanning instruments, and wearable devices, it will be possible to produce exact digital replicas of ourselves. It will also be possible to track each part of these digital replicas as they change and operate, so we can better monitor and manage our health.

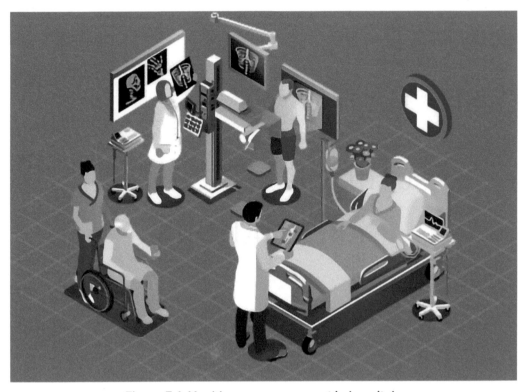

Figure 5-1 Healthcare management in hospitals

5.2 Smart Homes

Another area where digital twin has a significant impact is in smart home management (Figure 5-2). A digital twin enables building operators to integrate previously isolated systems, such as heating, ventilation, air conditioning (HVAC), pathfinding systems, etc., to make new decisions, optimize work processes, and perform remote monitoring. A digital twin can also be used to control the interior environment to enhance the resident experience.

By optimizing systems and connecting personnel using digital twins, owners and operators can lower operating and maintenance costs, raise utilization rates, and increase the overall value of assets. In fact, digital twin can help reduce the operating costs of certain buildings to as low as RMB 1.8/m^3 per year.[23]

Figure 5-2 Smart home management

Figure 5-3 Aircraft maintenance and support

5.3   Aerospace

In the aerospace field (Figure 5-3), the US Department of Defense was the first to apply digital twin technology to data flow and information mirroring in aerospace maintenance and support. First, a digital model of an actual aircraft was built. The model was then synchronized with the actual state of the aircraft using sensors. In this way, after every flight technicians can evaluate whether it needs to be serviced, based on the aircraft's current state and past payloads, and whether it could bear a certain mission payload.

5.4   Oil and Gas Exploration

In the field of oil and gas exploration (Figure 5-4), a high-tech company in China used its three core techniques of WEFOX (3D pre-stack migration imaging), GEOSTAR (storage layer prediction), and AVO-MAVORICK (3D oil and gas prediction) to achieve major breakthroughs in the development of software for oil and gas and geothermal energy processes. These include exploration and development, urban survey, 3D seismic data acquisition, image processing and interpretation, comprehensive geophysical and geological research, block resource evaluation, drilling and completion technical services, horizontal well fracturing design and execution, and its underground 3D space Big Data AI platforms (Figure 5-5). Digital twin technology combines oil and gas exploration technology with AI to build an underground 3D space Big Data platform, which can not only accurately assess the economics of underground oil, gas, and geothermal resources, but also greatly improves the accuracy of 3D underground exploration. It accomplishes this by integrating disciplines such as data acquisition, imaging, seismology, geology, and engineering, together with innovative fusion technology and highly efficient scientific management.

5.5   Smart Logistics

In the field of smart logistics, cutting-edge technologies such as digital twin large displays and sorting robots have helped the industry to informatize and become smarter, so parcels can reach any part of China within 24 hours. Many delivery companies have adopted cutting-edge technologies such as digital twin centers, large-scale sorting

Figure 5-4 Oil and gas exploration

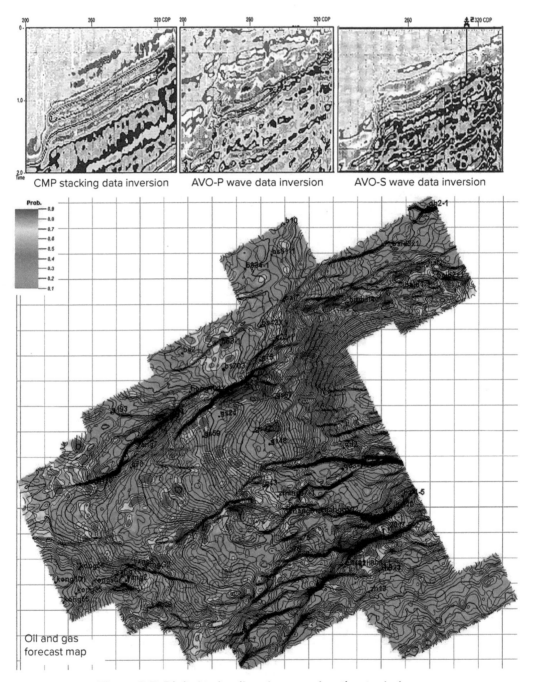

CMP stacking data inversion   AVO-P wave data inversion   AVO-S wave data inversion

Oil and gas forecast map

Figure 5-5 Digital twin oil and gas exploration techniques

systems, vehicle-mounted weighing scales, AR measuring, unmanned trucks, etc., to improve their service capabilities. Some companies have even spent more than RMB 500 million on digitalization and expect to spend RMB 3.5 billion annually in the years ahead on IT R&D, operation matching, backend management, and other aspects as they build digital twin centers.[24]

5.6   Promoting Real World Search

In the Internet age, search engines make it easier for people to discover, understand, and recognize stuff.

In the future, drones, autonomous vehicles, and sensors will replace the existing web crawlers. Search technology will become more complex, and we will be able to search for something based on smell, taste, vibration, texture, relative density, reflection, and air pressure.

Over time, new search engines will enable us to find almost anything online and offline. Everything will be transparent (Figure 5-6).

Figure 5-6 New search engines will promote real world search

5.7   Monitoring and Managing Brain Activity

The human brain is one of the most complex products of nature. Researchers in many countries are trying to use digital technology to unravel how we think. For example, Hewlett Packard is working on the Blue Brain project with the Swiss Federal Institute of Technology Lausanne. The project aims to build a digital model of the mammalian brain in order to discover its working principles, so the brain's movement, sensing, and management functions can be simulated using a large number of calculations. This would help in the diagnosis and treatment of brain diseases.

This also includes the revolutionary technology being explored and researched, brain-machine interface (BMI) technology. Particularly for implanted BMI devices, the monitoring and management of their operation's safety after implantation into the brain can be achieved through digital twin technology. This ensures the safety of BMI devices operating within the brain and enables early detection of potential issues or component improvements through effective early warning systems.

CHAPTER 6

DIGITAL TWIN APPLICATIONS

6.1 Aircraft Engine PLM Based on Digital Twin

The conventional model for developing aircraft engines can no longer meet the ever-increasing demands for engine performance and working range. A digital and smart development model, using IT as the engine, is the way to go. Even though digitalization has been talked about for a long time, it did not reach the sophistication level of digital twin. The construction of digital twins for aircraft engines has triggered disruptive innovations in the intelligent manufacturing and servicing of engines (Figure 6-1).

There is also a need to mention the AFRL in this respect. In 2011, this laboratory began using digital twin to estimate the remaining lifespan of aircraft fuselage and proposed a conceptual model for fuselage digital twins. This hyper-realistic model includes the tolerances and material microstructural characteristics of the actual aircraft manufacturing process. With the help of high-performance computers, the fuselage digital twin can be used to perform a large number of virtual flights before the aircraft takes off. This helps to detect unexpected failures, enabling design corrections. Sensors on the aircraft allow parameters (such as six-degree-of-freedom acceleration, surface temperature, pressure, etc.) to be collected during the flight. The input of such

Figure 6-1 Conceptual illustration of aircraft engine digital twins

data into the fuselage digital twin adjusts the model, which is then used to predict the remaining lifespan of the fuselage (Figure 6-2).

NASA experts are already working on a reduced order model (ROM) to predict the aerodynamic loads and internal stresses experienced by an airframe. Integrating this ROM into the fuselage lifespan prediction model enables high-fidelity stress failure prediction, structural reliability analysis, and structural life monitoring to improve the management of the aircraft body. Breakthroughs in these technologies would allow a low-fidelity digital twin to be built.

In addition, the AFRL has embarked on a structural mechanics project to study high-precision structural damage development and accumulation models. The AFRL Structural Sciences Center is studying multidisciplinary (thermal-dynamic-stress) models. As these technologies develop, they will be gradually integrated into the digital twin to improve its fidelity.

At the same time, the world's major aerospace manufacturers have proposed corresponding digital twin application models based on their businesses. They are committed to achieving in-depth interaction and integration between the virtual and real worlds in the field of aerospace, as well as promoting the transformation of their companies towards collaborative innovation in research, production, and services.

For example, GE is using or planning to use digital twin technology for the predictive maintenance and servicing of existing civilian-use turbofan engines and advanced turboprop engines (ATP) currently under development. Using large

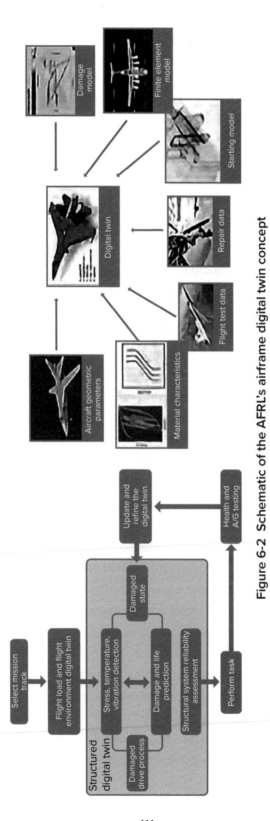

Figure 6-2 Schematic of the AFRL's airframe digital twin concept

amounts of sensor-collected data about flight, environment, and more, simulation is used to provide a comprehensive view of how the engines worked during flights. That allows them to determine wear and tear as well as when maintenance work should be carried out, thus achieving failure monitoring and prediction.

China's aerospace industry is also stepping up research on the industrial application of digital twin. The closed-loop, full-lifecycle, digital twin application framework for aerospace engines developed by scholars at the China Aerospace Engine Research Institute is shown in Figure 6-3.

There are five stages in the innovative application of aero engine digital twin technology:

1) Design phase. The development of aircraft engines is a typical example of complex system engineering. Problems include complexities in development requirements, system composition, product technology, manufacturing, testing and maintenance, project management, and working environment. Based on quantitative customer requirements (such as thrust-to-weight ratio, fuel consumption rate, surge margin, efficiency, reliability, etc.), the generic aero engine digital twin can be used to quickly build a complete simulation model of a customized new engine. Multi-system simulation can then be carried out on the new engine's digital twin to test its functions and overall performance. This would greatly improve the reliability of new product designs and is also a quick way to verify the design functions of new products.

2) Experimental phase. Conventionally, the development of aircraft engines depends primarily on physical testing. To test the characteristics and actual working performance of an engine, it is necessary to put together a test environment that approximates the actual working environment, such as on the ground and at high altitudes, and operating conditions of the engine, such as during flight. On the one hand, the design and optimization of tests take time, making testing time-consuming and costly. On the other hand, it may not be possible to recreate some extreme conditions with existing testing resources.

Based on the design-phase aero engine digital twin, a virtual testing system with a comprehensive set of test environments can be built. Based on quantitative test environment parameters, the model can be revised to optimize the tests. At the same time, engine performance in various scenarios can be predicted and underlying risks diagnosed, as the emphasis is placed on such "test flights."

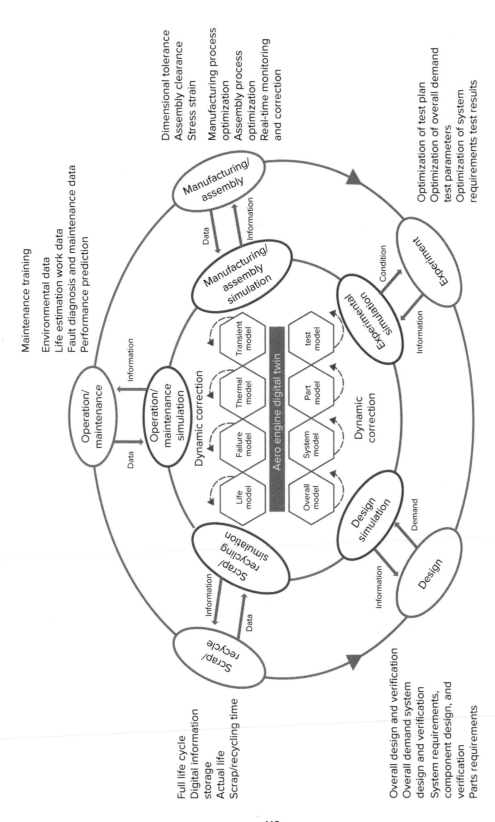

Figure 6-3 The closed-loop, full-lifecycle, digital twin application framework for aerospace engines developed by the China Aerospace Engine Research Institute

3) Manufacturing/assembly phase. Before the aircraft engine is manufactured and assembled, its digital twin can be used to optimize the manufacturing and assembly processes. During this phase, sensors can be used to collect information (such as dimensional tolerances, assembly gaps, stress and strain, etc.) in real time. Big Data technology is then used to regularly update the aircraft engine digital twin to ensure that it is a highly accurate reflection of reality. Using IoT, the manufacturing of engine parts can be monitored, corrected, and controlled in real time. This ensures that the processing of these parts meets standards and also produces personalized aircraft engine digital twins for the subsequent operation/maintenance phase.

4) Operation/maintenance phase. The engine, together with its digital twin, is delivered to the user concurrently. In this phase, Integrated Vehicle Health Management (IVHM) monitors the engine's operational parameters and working environment parameters, such as aerodynamics, heat, cycle load, vibration, stress and strain, temperature, pressure, humidity, air composition, etc. By mining the above-mentioned flight data, maintenance reports, and other recorded information, the digital twin regularly revises its simulation model so that it is possible to predict engine performance, perform fault diagnosis, and raise the alarm in real time. Using VR/AR and other technologies, experts and maintenance personnel can engage in immersive interaction to formulate maintenance plans and carry out virtual maintenance training.

5) Scrap/recycling stage. After the aircraft engine is scrapped or recycled, the digital twin containing data across its entire lifecycle can be stored forever. It can be used in the development of similar engines, forming a closed-loop engine lifecycle digital design and application model. This virtuous circle will greatly speed up the engine development process and improve the reliability of engine design.

Of course, many key technical problems need to be overcome to build an engine digital twin. Digital twin technology is a natural choice for reducing the time and cost of developing aircraft engines and for realizing intelligent manufacturing and service. Using data gathered throughout the engine's lifecycle, the engine digital twin dynamically adjusts its model to remain highly synchronized with the engine. This allows it to predict the engine's remaining lifespan and monitor its operating status. Additionally, since the digital twin manages the engine's data throughout its lifecycle, it can be used to develop similar products subsequently, thereby speeding up the development process and reducing development costs. As key technologies become available, the aircraft engine digital twin will become an important means of realizing digital design and manufacturing, as well as service guarantee, bringing both engine reliability and innovative design and manufacturing to a whole new level.

6.2   Assembly of Complex Products Based on Digital Twin

Associate Professor Liu Xiaojun and his team at the Southeast University of China have produced the following research outcomes on the assembly of complex products based on digital twins.

Complex product assembly is the final stage of and key link to realizing product function and performance. It is an important factor affecting the R&D quality and performance of complex products. The quality of assembly determines to a large extent the quality of the complex products. In industrialized countries, about a third of the manpower involved in product development is engaged in activities related to product assembly. Product assembly accounts for 20%–70% of the entire manufacturing workload. Rough estimates put the man-hours required for product assembly at 30%–50% of the total needed for production and development, with more than 40% of production costs spent on product assembly. The efficiency and quality of product assembly have a great impact on the product manufacturing cycle and quality.

As large, complex products such as spacecraft, aircraft, ships, and radars become smarter, more precisely made, and more reliant on optomechanics, their components become more complex. As a result, the assembly and adjustment of components is now a weak link in the development of complex products. Such products are characterized by having numerous types of components, having large changes in structural dimensions and irregular shapes, being produced singly or in small numbers, and having high assembly accuracy and coordination requirements. Their on-site assembly is generally regarded as a typical discrete assembly process. Even when all the components meet requirements, it is difficult for them to be assembled all at once. Multiple trials, repairs, adjustments, dismantling, and rework are needed before a qualified product is assembled. At present, with the widespread application of model-based definition (MBD) technology in the development of large complex products, the 3D model as the only data source of the whole life cycle of the product is effectively transmitted; it promotes the data unification of each link of "design–process–manufacture–assembly–test" life cycle of such products. This, in turn, has resulted in more attention being paid to assembly process design and on-site assembly applications based on 3D models.

3D model digital product process design connects MBD-based product design and manufacturing, while 3D digital assembly technology is an important part of product process design. 3D digital assembly technology is a deeper extension of virtual assembly technology. Without the need for physical samples and taking place in a 3D virtual environment, product assembly, disassembly, and maintenance are analyzed, verified, and optimized.

The assembly process—including sequence, path, precision, and performance—is also planned, simulated, and optimized to reduce the number of trial assemblies required in the product development process, thereby improving product assembly quality, efficiency, and reliability. In digital product process design, the MBD-based 3D assembly process model receives all the information of the 3D design model and transmits both model and process information to the subsequent manufacturing, testing, and maintenance phases. This is crucial for standardized data PLM and is also the basis for realizing model-driven intelligent assembly in the cyber-physical system of the assembly workshop.

The core strategy of Industry 4.0 and the Industrial Internet is the usage of cyber-physical systems for people, equipment, and products to be connected in real time, recognize each other, and communicate effectively, resulting in a highly flexible and intelligent manufacturing model. For the seamless integration of 3D assembly process design and on-site assembly applications for complex products, cyber-physical systems that enable smart assembly are the basis for realizing the smart assembly of complex products. One of the core issues is how to facilitate interaction between the physical and digital assembly processes, as well as how to blend them together.

With the rapid development of a new generation of infocommunication technologies (such as the IoT, Big Data, Industrial Internet, mobile Internet, etc.), and software and hardware systems (such as cyber-physical fusion systems, RFID, smart equipment, etc.), the emergence of digital twin technology will enable real-time connection between and integration of the virtual and the real, the effective integration and management of multisource heterogeneous data throughout the product lifecycle, and the optimization of various activities in the product development process. Therefore, using digital twin technology in the construction of a product assembly process model that connects and integrates the physical assembly workshop with the digital assembly world is the key to effectively reducing process and design changes, ensuring assembly quality, improving assembly success rates, and realizing intelligent assembly.

6.2.1 Basic framework

The assembly process driven by digital twin is based on linking the IoT of all equipment to achieve deep integration of the physical and digital worlds of the assembly process. Through intelligent software service platforms and tools, precise control over parts, equipment, and the assembly process is achieved. Through the unified and efficient management and control of the complex goods assembly process, the product assembly system is self-organizing, self-adapting, and dynamically responsive. The details are shown in Figure 6-4.

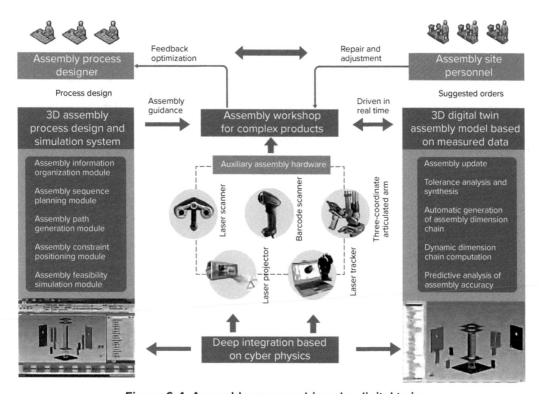

Figure 6-4 Assembly process driven by digital twin

By building a 3D assembly twin model, measured data from the assembly site is introduced. Using the model based on actual measurements, the assembly site and process can be simulated with high fidelity in real time. According to the actual implementation, the assembly outcome and the inspection results can be utilized to accurately provide repair suggestions and to optimize the assembly method in real time, providing an effective way to realize the scientific assembly of complex products and predictions of assembly quality. Intelligent assembly technology driven by digital twin will realize the interaction and integration between the virtual and physical worlds of the product assembly to build a cyber-physical system for the process of complex product assembly, as shown in Figure 6-5.

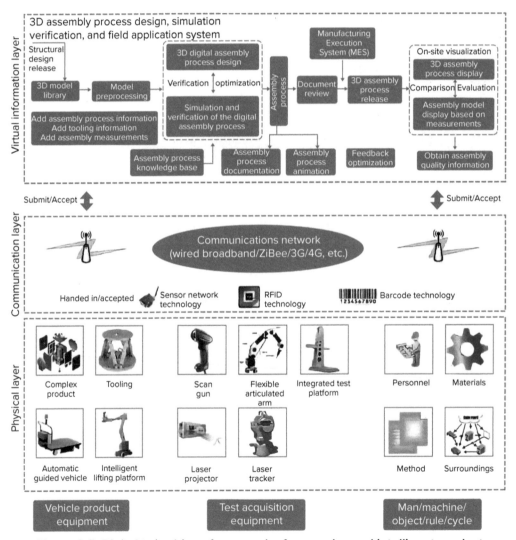

Figure 6-5 Digital twin-driven framework of a complex and intelligent product assembly system

6.2.2 Method(s) and characteristic(s)

Most existing digital assembly process design methods are based on ideal digital models. Such models can be used in the assembly process design stage to check the assembly sequence, obtain the assembly route, and detect assembly interference. However, when it comes to the on-site assembly of large complex products that are manufactured singly or in small batches, current 3D digital assembly process designs are unable to cope adequately with real-time process plan changes such as on-site assembly repairs or adjustments. This is because components and assembly errors were not considered in the assembly process design. Table 6-1 shows the problems in the product assembly process design.

Table 6-1 Assembly process design phase problems caused by failing to consider components, assembly errors, etc.

1	Failing to fully consider physical information and measured data during the assembly process design stage
2	Failing to realize the deep integration of virtual assembly information and the physical assembly process
3	The existing 3D assembly process design cannot efficiently and accurately predict and optimize assembly accuracy

1) Failing to fully consider physical information and measured data during the assembly process design stage. The 3D assembly process design based on MBD technology provides a design method centered on process modeling and simulation. The integrated 3D model is used to fully convey the product definition and describe in detail the 3D model process (such as feasible assembly sequence and pathway), assembly dimensions, tolerance requirements, and auxiliary processes. However, the above model does not take into account the manufacturing process, let alone the evolution of the actual assembly process model. Therefore, the product assembly manufacturing process model is combined with the ideal digital model, and physical information is fully considered in the assembly process design stage to realistically simulate the physical assembly of complex products in order to raise the one-time assembly success rate.

2) Failing to realize the deep integration of virtual assembly information and the physical assembly process. Currently, virtual assembly technology is mainly based

on the analysis, simulation, and verification of the ideal geometric model assembly process. This raises the conundrum of how to apply it to the actual assembly. In terms of cumulative assembly errors and the effect of component parts' manufacturing errors on the assembly process, virtual assembly technology is lacking in analysis and foresight, making it inaccurate and unable to completely resolve engineering application problems during the manufacturing/assembly process. The crux of the above-mentioned problems is that the technology does not support the dynamic simulation, planning, and optimization of the assembly process and cannot realize the deep integration of virtual assembly information and the physical assembly process.

3) The existing 3D assembly process design cannot efficiently and accurately predict and optimize assembly accuracy. In the assembly of large complex products, repairs or adjustments are often carried out on the spot. The issues with 3D assembly process design include how to analyze the cumulative errors of the assembly process, how to predict product assembly accuracy before actual assembly occurs, and how to devise a reasonable and reliable assembly and adjustment plan based on actual dimensions collected at the assembly site. Currently, 3D assembly process design technology fails to account for factors such as the actual manufacturing precision of parts and geometric surface contact constraints, making it difficult to apply assembly accuracy estimates and optimization methods at the assembly site.

In summary, compared to traditional assembly, digital twin-driven product assembly is a transformation: from a virtual information assembly process to one that takes into account both virtual and physical information; from using theoretical design model data to using actual measurements in modeling; from single process elements to multidimensional process elements; and from an assembly process with digital guidance to one in which both physical and virtual assembly evolve together.

6.2.3 Key theories and technologies

To realize intelligent assembly driven by digital twin and to build cyber-physical systems for complex product assembly processes, critical breakthroughs are needed in the key theoretical and technical issues shown in Table 6-2.

Table 6-2 Key theories and technologies in digital twin-based product assembly process design

1	Digital twin assembly process modeling
2	Analyzing assembly precision and predicting assembly feasibility using integrated data
3	Deep integration of virtual and real assembly processes and application of process intelligence

1) Digital twin assembly process modeling. Study product assembly model reconstruction based on the measurements of parts and reconstruct the 3D models of parts in the product assembly model.

   Design the assembly process and optimize its simulation using the actual sizes of the processed parts. At the start, the research group studied assembly process design methods based on 3D models, including 3D assembly process modeling methods, assembly sequence planning, and assembly path definition methods in a 3D environment, as well as intelligent mapping methods between the assembly process structure tree and assembly process flow.

2) Analyzing assembly precision and predicting assembly feasibility using integrated data. Study methods to integrate assembly process physical and virtual data, establish methods to analyze whether the assembly of the parts will be successful and to predict the precision of these parts, and enable to the dynamic adjustment and real-time optimization of the assembly process. Research the construction of 3D digital twin assembly models based on actual assembly measurements, build 3D digital twin assembly models according to the actual assembly and measurements obtained in real time and achieve the deep integration of the 3D digital twin assembly model with the actual physical model in a virtual environment.

3) Deep integration of virtual and real assembly processes and application of process intelligence. Establish the expression mechanism of the 3D assembly process demonstration model, study the lightweight display technology of the 3D assembly model, and simplify the multilevel product 3D assembly process design and simulation process documents. Study on-site display methods of the 3D assembly process that are driven by physical entities of the assembly process so that assembly process information—such as the assembly models required on-site,

assembly dimensions, assembly resources, etc.—can be accurately displayed in real time. Study the association mechanism between physical objects on site and the 3D assembly process display models for the deep integration of assembly process flow, MES, and actual assembly information at the assembly site. Enable the intelligent delivery of assembly process information.

6.2.4   Examples of on-site assembly application platforms for parts

To collect information, manage data, and optimize control for the on-site assembly process of complex products, an intelligent digital twin platform comprising both software and hardware is built based on cyber-physical systems (Figure 6-6). The system provides real-time data from the assembly site for generating both digital twin assembly models and solutions for the optimization/adjustment of the assembly process.

I: Assembly department body (partial); II: articulated arm measuring equipment and industrial computer; III: laser tracker equipment and industrial computer; IV: laser projector equipment (group) and industrial computer; V: computer control platform and relevant software systems.

The on-site parts assembly application system includes hardware (such as the articulated arm measuring instrument, laser tracker, laser projector, computer control platform, etc.) and 3D assembly software (such as process design software, lightweight assembly demonstration software, etc.).

The product assembly process design workflow based on digital twin is as follows: First, the product 3D design model(s) and the measured-state data of structural parts are entered to perform pre-assembly operations such as assembly sequence planning, assembly path planning, laser projection planning, and assembly process simulation. An assembly sequence plan that involves the least amount of repair is then generated to reasonably coordinate the repair work with the assembly sequence. After it has been approved, the generated assembly process file is disseminated to the assembly workshop, where it is electronically displayed to guide workers in performing the actual assembly. Before actual assembly, the state of the initial parts is adjusted. Finally, with the aid of intelligent assembly hardware, the laser projection equipment (group) can efficiently and accurately generate the laser projection of product assembly activities. In order to prevent errors and reduce the likelihood of multiple assembly attempts, the laser tracker can collect on-site assembly deviations in real time to inform the process design. Following assembly deviation analysis and assembly accuracy prediction, an adjustment plan is produced for the assembly. This ensures high-quality product assembly.

At present, there are research groups that have completed part of the exploration work in 3D assembly process modeling, 3D assembly process design, and lightweight assembly process demonstration. The next stage involves looking at engineering applications. As for digital twin-driven 3D assembly process application, intelligent assembly platform construction, cross-system and cross-platform software, and hardware integration, these are still in the initial research phase and further research needs to be carried out.[25]

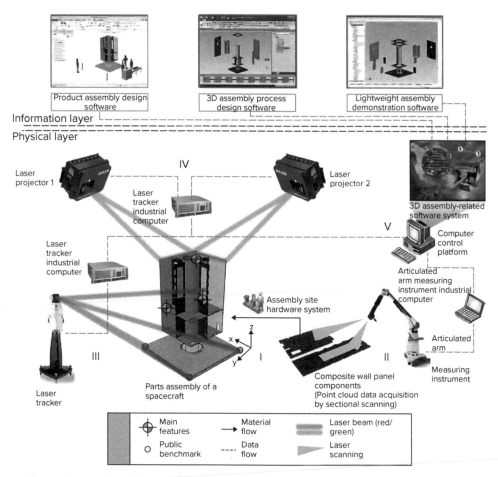

Figure 6-6 An intelligent digital twin software and hardware platform based on cyber-physical systems

6.3   APEX, BP's Advanced Simulation and Surveillance System

Building digital twins of our bodies to test the effect(s) of different options on our arteries, veins, and organs is certainly a fascinating and tempting proposition. This is the concept behind APEX, BP's advanced simulation and surveillance system, which creates a virtual copy of BP's production systems around the world.

Let us learn about how APEX helps BP optimize production and increase value, especially in terms of shortening operation time.

Anyone who knows a little about oil extraction would know that crude oil molecules have billions or even trillions of different flow paths through oil extraction equipment. Take BP's huge North Sea oil fields as an example. Every day, more than 200,000 barrels of crude oil flow from seabed rocks through thousands of kilometers of wellbores and risers into a complex pipeline network and crude oil processing infrastructure. At the core of these operations are BP engineers, who have decisions to make every day. Using complex calculations, they determine which valves to open, how much pressure to apply, and how much water to inject. All these are done to optimize production safely.

But traditional decision-making methods are complex and tedious, even as they remain essential for continuous improvement of performance and productivity. Previously, engineers relied on their skills and experience, but now they can also count on digital twin technology, especially digital cloning technology. This cutting-edge simulation and surveillance system established using digital twin technology can digitally reproduce every element of the actual facilities. BP's North Sea oil fields have always been at the forefront of digital development, and the APEX system developed there has been rolled out to the company's global production systems.

North Sea oil fields petroleum engineer Giuseppe Tizzano explained: "APEX is a production optimization tool that makes use of integrated asset models. But, it is also a formidable surveillance tool that can be used in the field to spot issues before they have major effects on production."

The lifeblood of APEX is the data, flow pattern, and pressure information from BP's oil wells. Its structure is a hydraulic model. Like human bodies, the APEX system is responsive and sensitive. With APEX, production engineers can run optimization simulations that used to take hours in just a few minutes. For example, Carlos Stewart, a petroleum engineer in the Gulf of Mexico, shared that "Engineering time has been the biggest payback—a system optimization could take 24–30 hours. In APEX, it takes 20 minutes." After adopting the system, BP's global production increased by 30,000 barrels in 2017.

In addition, the system can also be used to safely test hypothetical scenarios. By matching the model with actual data, hourly tests can be carried out to detect abnormal conditions, and the factor(s) of the analysis can be simulated to show engineers how to adjust the flow rate, pressure, and other parameters to safely optimize production.

Since some of BP's most complex production systems are located in the North Sea, the APEX system was first tested in multiple oil fields there. Today, Tizzano is part of a team that provides expert advice worldwide because APEX is now being used at other oilfields. Those areas are benefiting from the system's incredible ability to determine how efficiency can be improved and predict where potential problems lie.

The feedback from the production team has been positive. Amy Adkison, optimization engineer at BP, said: "We weren't sure we could use APEX on the North Slope because of the sheer scale of routing options, but we've had great support incorporating that complexity. We're excited to be able to collaborate with the other regions on the same technology platform." She also said, "Each one has solved a puzzle for their region and we're eager to share learnings to boost optimization. It's meant that we have deployed in months instead of years."

Shaun Hosein, BP's head of system optimization in Trinidad and Tobago, explained, "There is always some kind of activity in such a large system—wells starting up, valve testing, pipeline inspections and so on. Using our new tools, we can now quickly simulate what will happen, so we can optimize production."

Hosein added, "In one case, we had to shut in a pipeline for maintenance at our onshore facility, which would previously have meant lost production—but the system simulated the procedure and showed us exactly how to re-route the flows and at what speeds. It protected a large volume of production for the three days it took to complete the maintenance."[26]

Therefore, there are good reason to believe that APEX will account for an increasing portion of BP's global investment portfolio. In the years ahead, the APEX system will definitely create greater value for BP.

6.4 Comprehensive Enterprise Budgeting Systems Based on Digital Twin

Commercially, digital twin technology refers to the cross-domain integration of technologies such as the IoT, real-time communication, 3D design, and simulation analysis modeling to provide the virtual world with feedback from equipment.

Digital twin can also be applied to enterprise management. In their informatization journey, many Chinese companies have adopted business systems to manage their finances, inventory, and human resources, and for office automation (OA) and customer relationship management (CRM). Within a company, these systems and their data are isolated from each other. Even if there is a master set of data that has been tidied up, real-time connectivity between the various business systems in a company is still difficult to achieve. This makes it very difficult for the company's management to have a complete picture of business operations in a timely manner. Most existing enterprise management software aims to simulate business processes and offline business operations in the form of documents, forms, processes, etc., rather than establish a digital model of the business. Therefore, a large amount of data redundancy is generated, and data consistency is poor.

Multidimensional data warehouse software and applications cater to such scenarios. With a history of 30 years, multidimensional data warehouse technology mainly uses multidimensional modeling to help a company "unify" its data during its informatization journey. It has become a powerful tool for building digital twin(s) for enterprise management.

In practical applications, the multidimensional data warehouse analyzes business data in real time by creating a multidimensional model of the company's business operations. It also forecasts business outcomes based on drivers, provides early warning of risks, and makes timely adjustments. Enterprise Performance Management (EPM) is a typical tool for building a dynamic model of enterprise management, and multidimensional data warehousing is at its core. In an enterprise's IT architecture, business systems such as Enterprise Resource Planning (ERP) provide EPM with data.

As multidimensional data warehousing and distributed computing develop, EPM is likely to replace traditional business systems like ERP for the real-time integration of data generation, modeling and data collection, analysis and early warning generation, and decision-making support. In the informatization of comprehensive enterprise budgeting management, enterprise management digital twins built using multidimensional data warehouses will help companies integrate their planning and budgeting management, execution and control, and analysis and decision-making. Figure 6-7 shows the architecture of the EPM application.[27]

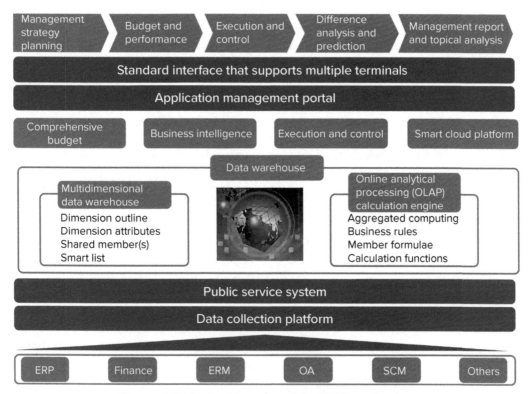

Figure 6-7 The architecture of the EPM application

6.5   Construction and Application of China's First In-Service Oil and Gas Pipeline Digital Twin

As the pace of building China's oil and gas backbone pipeline network quickens, and against a backdrop of rapid development and application of new information technologies, such as the IoT, Big Data, cloud computing, and AI, PetroChina has come up with a smart pipeline construction model that would provide fully-digitized handover, intelligent operations, and full-lifecycle management. The China-Myanmar pipeline was chosen as a pilot for the digital reconstruction of in-service pipelines. The China-Myanmar pipeline is an in-service mountain pipeline with oil and gas pipelines in parallel. It involves crude oil and natural gas stations and valve chambers. The crude oil pipeline is a complete hydraulic system. In this pilot project, the design, procurement, and construction during the building of the pipeline and part of the operation and maintenance data were reconstructed. 3D laser scanning, tilt-shift photography, and 3D digital modeling were used to construct a digital twin for the pilot-testing section of the China-Myanmar oil and gas pipeline. This has built the data foundation for the intelligent operation of the pipeline.

6.5.1 Digital twin building

The construction of a digital twin for the in-service oil and gas pipeline targets the route and stations. The process is divided into four parts: data collection, data verification and alignment, entity and model reconstruction, and data transfer. For now, the digitally reconstructed route and stations are submitted to the PCM system (natural gas and pipeline ERP engineering construction management subsystem) and PIS (pipeline integrity management system). After the data center is completed, there would be a formal handing over (Figure 6-8).

The first three parts of the process are described below.

6.5.1.1 Data collection

For the pipelines to operate normally, it is necessary to determine the scope of digital reconstruction, which mainly includes proximity environmental data, design data, and pipeline completion data. Environmental data includes basic data on the geography and topography around the pipelines to establish the environmental bearing capacity for the pipeline itself. The design data includes special evaluation data, identification data of the initial high-consequence areas, and construction drawings design data.

Construction completion data includes completion measurements, pipeline rerouting and associating construction and procurement data with the pipeline body.

Of the existing data, mainly the completion drawing, procurement, and construction data are collected in order to analyze the completeness and accuracy of existing results (such as completion measurements, midline data, basic geographic information, etc.). Through sampling and checking the scope, consistency, spatial reference system, and accuracy of the existing data, personnel carry out collection and verification to determine the scope and means of collecting supplementary data. Based on the analysis of existing data, they quantify data reconstruction indicators (Table 6-3). It is then possible to supplement data collection using reference points, pipeline midline detection, pipeline signage survey, aerial photogrammetry, basic geographic information, 3D laser

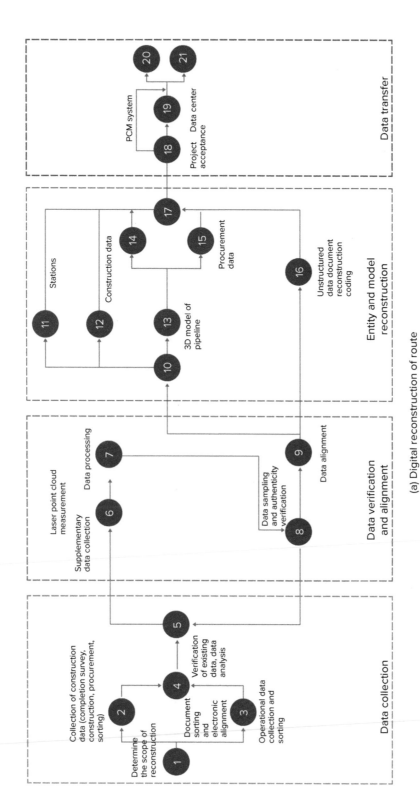

(a) Digital reconstruction of route

Figure 6-8 Flowchart for building an in-service pipeline digital twin

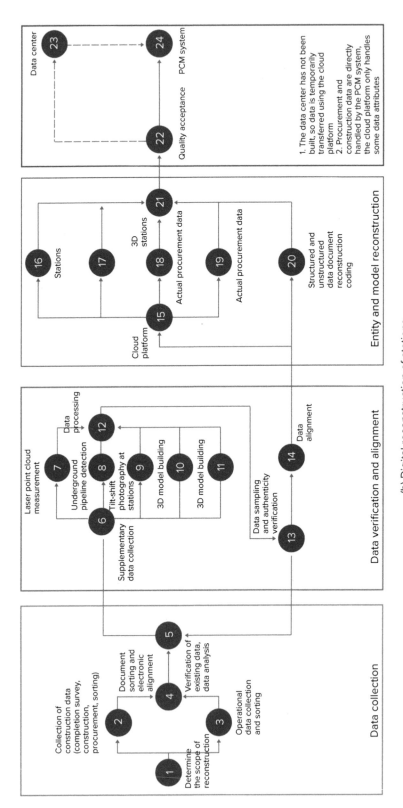

(b) Digital reconstruction of stations

Figure 6-8 (Continued)

scanning, 3D terrain construction, tilt-shift photography at stations, station pipeline detection, key equipment nameplates, etc.

Table 6-3 Technical indicators for the digital reconstruction of in-service pipelines

Indicator	Requirement
Basic geographic information data collection	400 m on each side of the center line
Satellite remote sensing image	At least 2.5 km on both sides, the resolution is not less than 0.5 m or 1 m, and precision should meet the requirements of 1:10,000
Aerial photogrammetry orthophotograph	400 m on each side, the resolution is greater than 0.2 m
Aerial photogrammetry digital elevation model	400 m on each side of the pipeline
High-precision 3D scanning of large crossing points	For large-scale crossings, the distance between target points should not be less than 0.02 m. For general regions, the distance between target points should not be less than 0.05 m, and the distance between other points should not be less than 0.10 m

6.5.1.2 Data verification and alignment

Data verification and alignment is a key step in turning data into information. In this step, pipeline ancillary facilities and surrounding environmental data are verified and aligned based on girth weld information or information of entities with unique geographic coordinates. Alignment is based on relatively precise data, so that the pipeline attributes during construction are associated with detection outcomes during operation and the surrounding features of the pipeline. Data verification and alignment primarily involve the centerline, the welded parts, the pipelines (including underground ones), cables, and auxiliary facilities in stations.

For ordinary pipelines, underground pipeline detectors and GPS equipment are used to locate the centerlines. Retesting, drilling, and excavation are used to verify such data. At river crossings, a fixed electromagnetic induction coil is used to measure the distribution of AC signals above pipelines, in order to locate their locations based on attenuation. In this pilot, underwater burial depth measurement was carried out at the

Shweli River. Digital design software was used on completion measurements to produce a profile view of the pipeline. This was compared with detection results to determine the location of the pipelines and their elevation.

The internal inspection of welded parts of the China-Myanmar pipeline uses mileage and pipe length to align the weld seams and combines welding data from the internal inspection and construction records. Using pipe bends as segments, alignment is carried out and missing weld locations and recording errors are rectified.

The pipelines and ancillary facilities in stations are verified and aligned by comparing the 3D model with the on-site laser point cloud model.

Workers then investigate and measure obvious points, such as telecommunication wells, to find out the type, direction, and buried depth. For hidden points, underground pipeline detectors are used to detect their buried depth and attributes, using real-time dynamic positioning or marking the pipeline point coordinates using collected information to produce a topographic map of pipeline points, pipeline direction, locations, and connections. The 3D model plan is compared with the survey results to verify the deviation of the pipeline position and buried depth.

6.5.1.3 Entity and model reconstruction

1) Pipeline. The reconstruction of the line model is based on measurement data at completion. Data verification and alignment are then performed to produce the data required for building the pipeline model.

   There are three main types of crossings: excavation, suspension cable, and mountain tunnel. For excavation, the entity comprises the pipeline and hydraulic protection and is reconstructed in the same way as the line. For suspension cable, the structural entities include the main tower, bridge deck, pipe anchor, bridge pier, and pipeline support. 3D laser point cloud scanning is used to obtain a complete model of the spanning bridge. For mountain tunnels, due to the complexity of the main tunnel structure and the spanning bridge structure, the model has to be constructed by combining the 3D laser scanning point cloud data. For mountain tunnels and portals, the laser point cloud method is used to gather data of the actual set-up. As for the tunnel body and other relevant components, Revit software is used to model and correlate the data collected during construction and upon completion.

2) Station(s). Station entity and model reconstruction are completed using 3D data-bases, the Revit family library, Process & Instrument Diagram (P&ID), Revit drawing, 3D models, and 3D general drawing models.

Through P&IDs, the content of system diagrams and reports are structured. Smart P&ID design is carried out using SPP&ID software. Design data is integrated into the system using SmartPlant Foundation (SPF) software as the data management platform, and the integration of SmartPlant Instrument (SPI) and SmartPlant 3D (SP3D) software establishes a shared project database and document library to complete the construction of a 3D database.

Data verification is carried out using the 3D laser point cloud data of the stations and valve rooms, as well as photographs, so that completion drawings and design changes are used as the basis for building the database. Laser point cloud measurement data is used as a verification method to establish the 3D data model of the station valve rooms. Revit software and completion drawings are used to build a 3D architectural model.

Using the surveyed terrain data, a 3D terrain model is used to build a 3D design site model. Cross-section information in detailed drawings of the structure allows for the establishment of linear structure components and models, as well as the non-linear structure models of the general drawing. The 3D terrain model is imported into the 3D design platform along with the 3D design site model and linear structure models of the general drawing. Key coordinate points, elevation, structural information of structures, key features around the stations, and other 3D scene data are entered to construct the 3D station database.

6.5.2   Main digital reconstruction techniques

6.5.2.1 Measuring reference points

A series of highly precise reference points are usually laid down within the measurement area prior to taking measurements. The D-level accuracy of GPS measurement is used at a frequency of one per 50 km to construct a surveying and mapping datum control network.

GPS single-point positioning accuracy is subject to multiple errors, including satellite ephemeris error, satellite clock error, atmospheric delay, receiver clock error, or multipath effect. The pipeline in the pilot test is in a mountainous area, with high mountains and dense forests that pose transportation and communication difficulties, which affect GPS positioning accuracy. To minimize errors, Precise Point Positioning (PPP) technology is used to obtain high-precision coordinate data as well as precise GPS satellite ephemerides and precise clock offset provided by the International GNSS Service (IGS) organization. Using a dual-band dual-frequency GPS receiver to measure positioning data for 38 high-precision reference points within nearly 700 km greatly improves operating efficiency and provides high accuracy and reliability.

6.5.2.2 Centerline detection

The centerline is the core of the pipeline integrity data model and the benchmark for the positioning and displaying of other basic data. Before detection, the number of elbows, angles, and directions in the completion data and internal detection data are sorted out as the basis for detection in order to improve detection accuracy. During detection, radio detection and Continuously Operating Reference Stations-Real Time Kinematic (CORS-RTK) techniques are used to complete underground pipeline detection. The scope, area, and number of points for pipelines are huge, located in mountainous regions, rivers, underwater, or within hazardous terrain, making conventional measurement techniques costly and potentially imprecise. Therefore, the CORS-RTK technique is used for field surveys to measure the coordinates and elevation of the centerline.

CORS-RTK is a real-time, dynamic positioning-measurement technique based on carrier phase observations, which can provide real-time 3D coordinates of a GPS mobile station in a specific coordinate system, with centimeter-level accuracy within the effective measurement range. After the collection of measurement data, automatic storage, and calculation are carried out. The computed measurement results are then compared with the completion centerline results, and the proportion of errors can be classified according to certain tolerances. The causes of errors are then analyzed together with the on-site situation to further improve the accuracy of detection data.

6.5.2.3 Aerial photogrammetry

Fixed-wing drones are used for pipeline aerial photogrammetry, with data interpretation carried out to obtain high-precision aerial photography. Various aerial photography zones are demarcated according to pipeline direction, terrain undulations, and flight safety conditions. The route is designed based on pipeline direction or the direction of the main entity in the surveillance area.

The route is laid as straight as possible, keeping the centerline in the middle of the shooting frame to ensure coverage that is no less than 200 m on both sides of the centerline. After the flight, the collected data is processed according to image control points and the captured photos to produce a 0.2 m digital orthophoto map (DOM) and a 2 m digital elevation model (DEM).

Aerial photogrammetry is the basis for geographic information collection, hydraulic protection planning, and 3D terrain model construction. It can provide predictions for geological disasters and high-consequence areas and provide a more intuitive and convenient description of the terrain, vegetation cover, and road access for the routine maintenance of pipelines. This provides accurate data support for government documentation, emergency rescue, decision support, high-consequence area management, and maintenance.

6.5.2.4 3D laser scanning

3D laser scanning, also known as real-world replication, is a technique used to quickly obtain 3D spatial information. Using this technique, non-contact scanning is used to obtain target surface information, such as target position, distance, azimuth, zenith distance, and reflectivity.

Using a 3D laser scanner to replicate the bridges at major pipeline crossings enables high-definition and high-precision 3D modeling in the same proportion as the pipeline bridges (Figure 6-9). The FARO S 350 ground-based 3D laser scanner is used to scan major crossings at the Lancang River, Nu River, and Yangbi River.

Figure 6-9 3D model of a bridge crossing

Point cloud processing and 3D modeling were then carried out. The high-precision 3D model provides a realistic and reliable data source for the maintenance, reconstruction, design, and inspection of major crossings. 3D scanning of buildings, equipment, etc., at stations is carried out using the RIEGL VZ-1000 laser scanner, and

Nikon D300S cameras were used for image data collection. After data collection, point cloud data splicing and coordinates correction were performed using target points to improve accuracy, and a 3D laser point cloud model of the station was constructed. The point spacing and accuracy of the point cloud model had to meet the requirements of the Oil and Gas Engineering Surface 3D Laser Scanning Measurement Specifications.

Build 3D models consistent with the proportions of pipeline bridges, buildings, and equipment through 3D laser scanning to achieve digital visualization. This is valuable for the digital management of stations, geological disasters, high-risk sections, and high-consequence areas.

6.5.2.5 3D terrain map construction

The construction of 3D maps for the terrain along the pipeline requires the integration of satellite and aerial images. The satellite images are 0.5–1 m resolution remote sensing images taken by the Gaofen-2 and GaoJing-1 satellites and a digital elevation model with a grid spacing of 30 m. The aerial images are DOM and DEM, taken using aerial photogrammetry. The 3D terrain map construction provides an overview of the terrain within 5 km of the pipeline, with a focus on terrain within 800 m, to support pipeline safety decision-making.

6.5.2.6 Oblique photogrammetry of stations

Oblique photogrammetry means that aerial remote sensing images are no longer restricted to the vertical direction. This is the main way 3D models of the stations are built. Hopong hexarotor drones collect multi-angle information about the stations, recording parameters such as altitude, speed, direction, and coordinates. The GPS RTK method is used to complete station image control point measurement, perform quality inspections by comparing original photos with the results of image control points, and process internal operational data to construct 3D tilt models of stations, 3D station topography, and built-in structures, equipment, and facilities of the stations.

6.5.3   Research outcomes and development of applications

6.5.3.1 Research outcomes

Digital reconstruction of the China-Myanmar oil and gas pipelines form a pipeline data asset library. This is used to build a digital twin that provides data support for pipeline operation and maintenance. It is a new technical means for the interaction and integration of information between real and virtual pipeline systems.

1) Pipeline data asset library. The pipeline data asset library integrates multisource, heterogeneous GIS, building information modeling (BIM), management information system (MIS), and CAD. A hybrid structure of client/server (C/S), browser/server (B/S), and mobile apps is employed to display basic geographic information around the pipeline, environmental data, and pipeline attribute data on the client side and to provide quick query functions.

Through the pipeline data asset library, basic geographic information on nearby resources available for development and sensitive areas around the pipeline can be queried. The centerline in construction design drawings and the completion centerline can be loaded on the same map, for a visual comparison of routing changes at different stages before analyzing the reasons behind them. Specific welds can be located for their serial numbers, anti-corrosion information of the pipe section before and after the weld, condition of the elbow(s), and buried depth of the pipeline to be queried. The position of crossings can be specified for querying the crossing method and protection form. Position, materials, and size parameters of the hydraulic protection can be detailed, so the effectiveness of hydraulic protection can be evaluated from information on the surrounding terrain and water systems. The pipeline data asset library is the data source for the identification of high-consequence areas and pipeline inspection management. It also provides a variety of basic data services for pipeline operation and maintenance.

2) Station data asset library. This asset library provides basic data for pipeline operation and maintenance, as well as for equipment management systems. It associates 3D models, 2D drawings, and structured data with unstructured documents for data interaction and sharing. It adopts relational database storage and uses the hardware-as-a-service cloud model. It has a three-tier architecture of data collection, processing, and application, is scalable, and has standardized service interfaces. It supports 3D model display, data query, and document retrieval, providing data support for intelligent pipeline applications. Integrating station tilt photogrammetry, 3D laser point cloud, and 3D data models, users are able to remotely view the station and its exterior.

Taking the digital reconstruction of the Baoshan Station as an example, its asset library contains environment data of the surroundings within 50 m of the station, as well as data on the station's processes, instruments, power supply, communications, architecture, general maps, cathodic protection, thermal engineering, HVAC, fire protection, water supply, and drainage. Above-ground process equipment, building structural models, and the building foundation, pipework, and cables were digitally reconstructed to establish a relationship between data, models, and unstructured documents. This resulted in mutual references between structured documents, such as plans, flow charts, and single-line pipe diagrams.

6.5.3.2 Development of applications

1) Multisystem integration. Multisystem integration is used for in-depth exploration of data value and the elimination of information silos. Using the platform-as-a-service (PaaS) concept, the base layer is displayed using the data layer, providing a platform and support for the data mounting display, as well as application docking and development of various systems.

   The digital twin is integrated with the SCADA system and video surveillance system for the visualization of real-time data and video surveillance data in mounted displays to aid operational management (Figure 6-10). Using http message interconnection and service interconnection integrated with ERP systems and equipment management systems, 3D results are combined to complete equipment disassembly and develop simulation applications for training, thereby catering to the training needs of employees. Data reconstruction is used to build a suitable production operation management system that is compatible with intelligent pipeline operations. Disaster monitoring and early warning systems are used

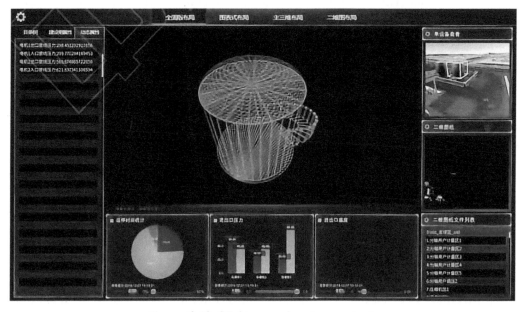

Figure 6-10 3D image of a storage tank

together with pipeline data, information on high-consequence areas, and disaster data points for real-time and dynamic analysis to provide early warnings. This results in an application that calculates the likelihood of disasters and supports decision-making in post-disaster management.

2) Guide maintenance and emergency rescue. During maintenance and repair operations, the pipeline digital twin can provide data support for the formulation of oil drainage plans for hot work and plugging operations, using information such as pipeline elevation, buried depth, and pipe materials. During excavation operations, it is easier to visually identify the location of hidden structures, such as underground pipes and cables. A combination of online monitoring and remote fault diagnosis is used to draw up a preventive maintenance plan based on risk and reliability. Through display of the results in 3D, equipment disassembly can be simulated, and equipment maintenance or repair plans can be formulated.

In emergency management, the steps in the emergency plan can be digitized according to the emergency repair process and linked to operations such as data query, path analysis, and buffer zone analysis to develop a digital emergency response plan. Personnel can simulate emergencies and follow the procedures of the plan to verify whether the plan meets emergency rescue needs. The system can automate the analysis of pipeline explosion impact range, oil contamination on waterways and buffer zones, etc., for pipelines with different transport media so as to build an accident or disaster impact analysis model. A digitally reconstructed water system and area data are used to build a leakage diffusion model for studying how water pollution changes after oil spills and emergency measures.[28]

CHAPTER 7

THE CHALLENGES AND DEVELOPMENT TRENDS OF DIGITAL TWIN TECHNOLOGY

7.1 New Trends in the Development of Digital Twin Technology

The digital twin is an inevitable product of technological development. It is inevitable based on the integration and mirroring of physical and virtual space for better and more efficient control of production, application, and other aspects of lifecycle management. As the relevant theories and technologies develop and demand continues to rise, there are six new trends in the development and application of digital twin technology, as shown in Table 7-1.

Table 7-1   New trends in the development of digital twin technology

1	Application field expansion requirements
2	Deep integration with new IT
3	Cyber-physical integration data requirements
4	Smart services requirements
5	Universal industrial interconnection
6	Dynamic, multidimensional, multitemporal, and spatial scale model requirements

7.1.1   Application field expansion requirements

When the digital twin concept was first introduced, it mainly catered to the military, aerospace, and aircraft industries to provide real-time control and monitoring of spatial technology for physical entities. In recent years, it has also found civilian use in power generation, automobiles, medical care, ships, oil and gas exploration, construction, and manufacturing, for example. Now, the technology has broad market prospects. The primary challenge in applying digital twin technology to these areas is how to create a digital twin model according to application and business requirements. The lack of either a universal digital twin model or guidance on how to build digital twins has seriously hindered the application of digital twin technology in these fields.

Given the improvement of 5G technology, drone surveillance, infrared monitoring, computer software and hardware, etc.—coupled with the emphasis various countries are placing on the IoT and the Industrial Internet—and propelled by industrial needs, a group of digital twin engineers will surely be cultivated in the time to come. In the foreseeable future, these technologies and talent will make the application of digital twin technology a part of the Industrial Internet era.

7.1.2   Deep integration with new IT

The application of digital twin is inseparable from new IT (Table 7-2).

Table 7-2 How new IT supports digital twin application

1	Connecting and integrating virtual and real using the IoT
2	Digital twin data storage and shared services based on the cloud model
3	Data analysis and integration, and intelligent decision-making based on Big Data and AI
4	Virtual reality mapping and visualization based on VR and AR

Deep integration of digital twin with new IT is needed for the integration of cyber-physical systems and the "collection–transmission–processing–usage" of multisource, heterogeneous data. This is necessary for the integration of cyber-physical data, supporting two-way connections and real-time interaction between the physical and the virtual, for carrying out real-time process simulation and optimization, and for providing various intelligent services on demand.

There are many research reports on the integration of digital twin and new IT, such as the three-tier digital twin architecture based on "cloud, fog, and edge" (computing), digital twin service-based packaging methods, the digital twin and Big Data smart manufacturing model, the digital twin reference model based on cyber-physical systems, and virtual-real integration of and interaction between VR/AR twins.

Currently, more technologies need to be developed as a package for the application of digital twin. At the same time, such technologies are becoming more sophisticated. Application support technology for hardware, as well as software and model-based related computing and monitoring technologies, are helping to promote the application of digital twin in various fields.

7.1.3 Cyber-physical integration data requirements

Data-driven intelligence is the current international academic frontier and the development trend of application process intelligence, such as data-driven intelligent manufacturing, design, operation and maintenance, and simulation optimization. The related research on cyber-physical fusion data requirements is shown in Table 7-3.

Table 7-3   Research on cyber-physical fusion data requirements

1	It mainly relies on information space data for data processing, simulation analysis, virtual verification, operational decision-making, etc. It lacks consideration and support for small physical, real-time datasets of application entities (such as equipment real-time operating status, sudden disturbance data, transient abnormalities small datasets, etc.). Hence the simulation lacks fidelity.
2	It mainly relies on the actual data of application entities to carry out the empirical evaluation, analysis, and decision-making. It lacks the scientific backing of Big Data (such as historical statistical data, temporal and spatial correlation data, tacit knowledge data, etc.). It suffers from over-generalization.
3	Although part of the work considers and uses both information data and physical data, which can make up for the above shortcomings to a certain extent, in actual implementation, the two types of data are often isolated, lacking comprehensive interaction and deep integration, which results in inconsistency and poor synchronization. The real-time performance and accuracy of the results need to be improved.

Data is also the core driving force of the digital twin. Unlike conventional digital technology, digital twin focuses on cyber-physical data integration in addition to information data and physical data, to enable real-time interaction between information and physical space through the integration of cyber-physical data. This also provides consistency and synchronization for more real-time and accurate applications and services.

Based on current technological development, it can be said that digital acquisition techniques, even data collection techniques from complex physical spaces and entities, are becoming more mature. As 5G technology becomes more widely used, it will further aid data collection and resolve the issues of real-time interaction, consistency, and synchronization between information and physical space. The basic technology for real-time, two-way interaction between the virtual and the real is already in place.

7.1.4   Smart services requirements

As digital twins becomes more widely used, the needs of different fields, different levels of users (such as on-site terminal operators, technicians, decision-makers, and end users), and different businesses for smart services have to be met (Table 7-4).

Table 7-4   Research related to smart service requirements

1	Virtual assembly, equipment maintenance, process debugging, and other on-site operational guidance service requirements
2	Specialized technical service requirements such as dynamic optimal scheduling of complex production tasks, dynamic manufacturing simulation, self-optimizing configuration for complex processes, and adaptive adjustment of equipment control strategies
3	Intelligent decision-making services such as data visualization, trend forecasting, demand analysis, and risk assessment
4	Oriented to the product end-user experience, immersive interaction, remote operation, and other requirements for foolproof and convenient service

Therefore, how to convert the various data, models, algorithms, simulations, results, etc., required in the application of digital twins to software or mobile apps that provide users with smart services is another challenge in the development of digital twins.

What is foreseeable is that, as smart manufacturing develops, Internet entrepreneurship will gravitate towards manufacturing, or more specifically, smart manufacturing and high-end manufacturing. As the IoT becomes the new industry buzzword, it will to a certain extent promote research into digital twin services and applications.

7.1.5   Universal industrial interconnection

Universal industrial interconnection (including the interconnection and collaboration between physical entities, physical and virtual entities, two-way communication and closed-loop control between physical entities and data/services, integration and fusion of virtual entities, data, and services, etc.) is the cornerstone for realizing virtual-real interaction and the integration of digital twins. Achieving universal industrial interconnection is the prerequisite for the application of digital twin.

At present, some researchers have begun to explore real-time interconnection methods for digital twins, including the Industrial Internet Hub for the real-time collection and integration of multisource, heterogeneous data for intelligent manufacturing; real-time communication and data exchange based on AutomationML

145

for information systems; remote interaction between on-site equipment, models, and users based on MTConnect; and the interconnection of and communication between physical and virtual entities through middleware. The development of 5G technology will, to a certain extent, facilitate two-way information interaction between the virtual and the real.

7.1.6 Dynamic, multidimensional, multitemporal, and spatial scale model requirements

Models drive digital twin to be applied. Currently, digital modeling for physical entities mainly focuses on the construction of geometrical and physical dimensional models and lacks multidimensional, dynamic models that can simultaneously reflect the geometry, physics, behavior, rules, and constraints of physical entities.

In terms of multiple dimensions, there is a lack of multiple spatial scale models that describe the attributes, behaviors, and characteristics of physical entities with different granularities using different spatial scales. At the same time, there is a lack of multi-time-scale models that use different time scales to describe how physical entities evolve with time. They accordingly cannot account for real-time, dynamic operation, the external environment, or the effects of interference.

In addition, from a system perspective, there is a lack of integration and fusion between models of different dimensions, spatial scales, and time scales. The problem of inadequate and incomplete models means that existing models of virtual entities are unable to truly and objectively describe and portray physical entities, leading to inaccurate results (such as simulations, predictions, evaluations, and optimization outcomes).[29]

Therefore, as digital twin technology is relatively new, its development for civil usage suffers from a lack of relevant models and data for multi-dimensional applications in physical space. How to go about building models that are dynamic, multidimensional, multitemporal, and multispatial scale is the current technical challenge for the development and practical application of digital twin technology.

7.2 The Five-Dimensional Model of Digital Twin

In order to adapt to new trends and demands, solve the problems encountered in the application of digital twin and enable digital twins to be applied in more fields, Beihang

University's digital twin technology research team expanded the existing 3D digital twin model to include two additional dimensions of digital data and service, leading to the innovative five-dimensional digital twin model. The group also studied the structure and application criteria of the five-dimensional model.[30]

The formula for the five-dimensional digital twin model is as follows:

$$M_{DT} = (PE, VE, Ss, DD, CN)$$

PE stands for physical entity, VE stands for virtual entity, Ss stands for service, DD stands for digital data, and CN stands for connections between the components.

Based on the above formula, the structure of the five-dimensional model is shown in Figure 7-1.

The five-dimensional model is able to satisfy the new requirements of digital twin application described in the previous section.

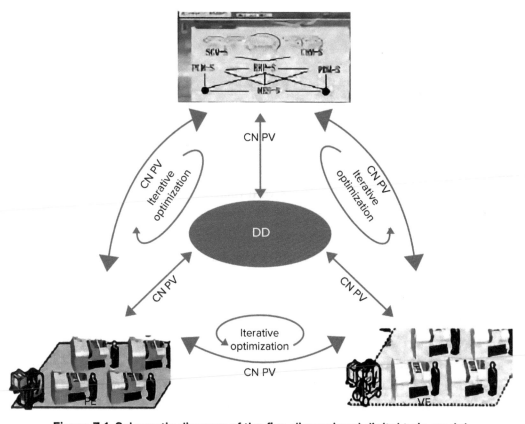

Figure 7-1 Schematic diagram of the five-dimensional digital twin model

First of all, M_{DT} is a general architecture that can be applied to different scenarios in different fields. Secondly, its five-dimensional structure can be integrated with new IT, such as the IoT, Big Data, and AI, to meet the needs of cyber-physical system integration, cyber-physical data integration, and virtual and real two-way connection and interaction. Finally, digital twin data integrates information and physical data to satisfy the consistency and synchronization requirements of the information space and physical space to provide more accurate and comprehensive data support for all elements, processes, and operations.

Ss is the encapsulation of data, models, algorithms, simulations, results, etc., as a service for different fields, users at different levels, and different businesses in the application of digital twin. This takes the form of application software or mobile apps that provide users with convenient services on demand. CN provides the universal industrial interconnection between physical entities, virtual entities, services, and data, thereby supporting real-time interconnection and integration of virtual and real. VE describes physical entities from multiple dimensions, multiple spatial scales, and multiple time scales.

7.2.1 PE

PE is the foundation of the five-dimensional digital twin model. Accurately analyzing and effectively maintaining PE are the prerequisites for establishing the M_{DT}. PE is hierarchical and can be divided according to function and structure into three levels: Unit PE, System PE, and System of Systems PE. Taking the factory digital twin as an example, the equipment in the factory can be regarded as Unit PE, the smallest functional units; the production lines with their equipment configurations can be regarded as System PE, responsible for the manufacturing of specific components; while the factory with the various production lines can be regarded as System of Systems PE, a comprehensive and complex system in which materials, energy, and information flow, and which organizes, coordinates, and manages various subsystems. Classifying PEs according to application requirements and control granularity is the basis for the layered construction of the M_{DT}. For example, construct a Unit M_{DT} for the monitoring, failure prediction, and maintenance of a single device; construct a System M_{DT} to analyze and optimize the scheduling, schedule control, and product quality control of a production line; as for the entire factory, a System of Systems M_{DT} can be constructed to describe the interaction and coupling between various subsystems, so as to analyze and predict the evolution of the entire system.

7.2.2 VE

As shown in the formula below, VE includes geometric models (Gv), physical models (Pv), behavior models (Bv), and rules models (Rv). These models describe and characterize PEs using multiple time scales and spatial scales:

$$VE = (Gv, Pv, Bv, Rv)$$

Gv refers to 3D models describing the geometric parameters (such as shape, size, position, etc.) and relationships (such as assembly relationships) of a PE. It has good temporal and spatial consistency with the PEs. The rendering of details can make Gvs resemble PEs more closely. Gvs can be created using 3D modeling software (such as SolidWorks, 3DS MAX, ProE, AutoCAD, etc.) or equipment (such as a 3D scanner).

Pv builds on Gv to include information on the physical properties, constraints, and characteristics of PEs. Tools such as Ansys, Abaqus, Hypermesh, etc., can usually be used to simulate and describe dynamic mathematical approximations macroscopically and microscopically for the modeling, simulation, and analysis of structures, fluids, electric fields, and magnetic fields.

Bv describes the real-time response and behavior of PEs with different granularities and different spatial scales, resulting from the external environment and disturbances under different time scales and internal operating mechanisms. Examples include evolutionary behavior, dynamic functional behavior, performance degradation behavior, etc.

Creating a PE behavior model is a complex process that involves the construction of various models, such as problem, evaluation and decision models etc. To create Bvs, modeling methods such as finite state machines, Markov chains, neural networks, complex networks, and ontology-based modeling can be used.

Rv includes rules based on historically linked data, experience based on tacit knowledge, and the relevant standards and guidelines.

These rules grow, learn, and evolve over time to give VEs real-time judgment, evaluation, optimization, and prediction capabilities, so that beyond controlling and operating PE, they can also correct and standardize themselves. Rv can be obtained by integrating existing knowledge or using machine learning algorithms to continuously mine and generate new rules.

Through the assembly, integration, and fusion of the four types of models above, a complete VE corresponding to the PE can be created. At the same time, the consistency, accuracy, and sensitivity of the VE are confirmed through Verification, Validation and

Accreditation (VV&A) of the model to ensure that the VE is an accurate mapping of the PE.

In addition, VR and AR technologies can be used to realize the superposition and fusion display of VE and PE to enhance the immersiveness, authenticity, and interactivity of the VE. In the application of digital twin, the VE will be key to the interactive interface.

7.2.3 Ss

Ss refers to the service-based packaging of various data, models, algorithms, simulations, and results required in the application of digital twins, and supports FService in digital twins in the form of tool components, middleware, and module engines. At the same time, it supports BService that meets the needs of different fields, users, and businesses in the form of application software and mobile apps. FService provides support for the implementation and operation of BService. The main content of FService is shown in Table 7-5.

Table 7-5   The main content of FService

1	Model management service for VE Modeling and simulation services, model assembly and integration services, model VV&A services, model consistency analysis services, etc.
2	Data management and processing services for DD Data storage, packaging, cleaning, correlation, mining, integration, and other services
3	Comprehensive connection service for CN Data collection services, perception access services, data transmission services, protocol services, interface services, etc.

The main content of BService is shown in Table 7-6.

Table 7-6   The main content of BService

1	Operation guidance service for terminal operators Virtual assembly services, equipment repair and maintenance services, process training services

(Continued)

2	Professional technical services for technical personnel Multilevel energy consumption and multistage simulation evaluation service, equipment control strategy adaptive service, dynamic optimization scheduling service, dynamic process simulation service, etc.
3	Intelligent decision-making service for decision-makers Demand analysis service, risk assessment service, trend forecast service, etc.
4	Products and services for end users User function experience service, virtual training, remote maintenance service, etc. For users, such services are a black box that shields the internal heterogeneity and complexity of digital twins and provides users with standard input and output through application software, mobile apps, etc., thereby making it easier for users to utilize digital twin application, providing convenient, on-demand use.

7.2.4 DD

DD drives digital twins. As shown in the following formula, DD mainly includes PE data (Dp), VE data (Dv), Ss data (Ds), knowledge data (Dk), and fusion-derived data (Df):

$$DD = (Dp, Dv, Ds, Dk, Df)$$

Dp mainly includes physical element attributes data reflecting PE specifications, functions, performance, and relationships, as well as dynamic process data reflecting PE operating conditions, real-time performance, environmental parameters, sudden disturbances, etc., which can be collected using sensors, embedded systems, and data acquisition cards. Dv mainly includes VE-related data, such as geometrical dimensions, assembly relationships, location, and other geometric model-related data; material properties, loads, characteristics, and other physical model-related data; driving factors, environmental disturbances, operating mechanisms, and other behavioral model-related data; constraints, rules, associations, and other rules model-related data; as well as data on process simulation, behavior simulation, and process verification, evaluation, analysis, and prediction based on the above models. Ds mainly includes FService-related data (such as algorithms, models, data processing methods, etc.) and BService-related data (such as data on business management, production management, product management, market analysis, etc). Dk includes expert knowledge, industry standards, rules and constraints, reasoning and inferences, a database of commonly-used algorithms, and a model library. Df is derived data obtained after data conversion, preprocessing, classification, association, integration, and fusion of Dp, Dv, Ds, and Dk. Through the fusion of physical live data and multi-space-time related data, historical statistical data, expert knowledge, etc., cyber-physical fusion data is obtained, thereby reflecting more comprehensive and accurate information, achieving information sharing and adding value.

7.2.5   CN

CN connects the various M_{DT} components.

As shown in the following formula, CN includes the connection between PE and DD (CN_PD), the connection between PE and VE (CN_PV), the connection between PE and Ss (CN_PS), the connection between VE and DD (CN_VD), the connection between VE and Ss (CN_VS), and the connection between Ss and DD (CN_SD).

$$CN = (CN\_PD, CN\_PV, CN\_PS, CN\_VD, CN\_VS, CN\_SD)$$

where:

1) CN_PD enables the interaction between PE and DD. Sensors, embedded systems, data acquisition cards, etc., can be used to collect PE data in real time. The data is then transmitted to DD through MTConnect, OPC UA, MQTT, and other protocol specifications. After being processed in the DD, the data or instructions can be transmitted through the above-mentioned protocols back to the PE to optimize its operations.
2) CN_PV enables the interaction between PE and VE. The implementation method and protocols utilized here are similar to that for CN_PD. Real-time PE data is transmitted to VE for updating and correcting various digital models. VE simulation and analysis data is then converted into instructions and sent to the PE actuator for real-time PE control.
3) CN_PS enables the interaction between PE and Ss. The implementation method and protocols utilized here are similar to that for CN_PD. The collected real-time PE data is transmitted to Ss to update and optimize it. Ss produces operational guidance, professional analysis, and decision-making optimization outcomes that are provided to users through application software or mobile apps. PE is then regulated manually.

4) CN_VD enables the interaction between VE and DD. Through database interfaces such as JDBC and ODBC, simulation and other data generated by VE are stored in DD in real time.

On the other hand, fusion data, lifecycle data, and other data in DD are read in real time to drive dynamic simulation.

5) CN_VS enables the interaction between VE and Ss. The two-way communication between VE and Ss can be realized through software interfaces such as Socket, RPC, MQSeries, etc., to complete direct instruction transfer, data sending and receiving, message synchronization, etc.

6) CN_SD enables the interaction between Ss and DD. Similar to CN_VD, database interfaces like JDBC, ODBC, etc., are used to store Ss data in DD in real time and read historical data, rules data, common algorithms, and models in DD to support the operation and optimization of Ss.[31]

7.3 Fifteen Application Areas of the Digital Twin Five-Dimensional Model

Digital twin is a cutting-edge technology that has emerged in recent years, or rather, it has only found civilian applications in recent years. Digital twin is a simulation process which uses physical models and sensors to obtain data. The data mapping is completed in virtual space to reflect the lifecycles of the corresponding entities. It is a technology in which the virtual world mirrors the physical one. This is carried out by means of computer technology, with the aid of sensors and other forms of monitoring technology. In the future, digital twin technology will be able to replicate everything in the physical world.

The industrial usage of digital twin technology will produce great changes in product design, production, maintenance, and repair. Based on the research and exploration of digital twin technology, it is likely that the technology will be adopted in the following areas relatively quickly, helping the relevant industries develop quicker and more effectively.

They include satellite/space communication networks, ships, vehicles, power plants, airplanes, complex electromechanical equipment, stereoscopic warehouses, medical care, factories, smart cities, smart homes, smart logistics, construction, remote monitoring, and personal health management.

7.3.1 Satellite/space communication networks

Satellites, as the most numerous, widely used, and rapidly developing spacecraft, are changing human lives and influencing human civilization. In recent years, the satellite industry has experienced rapid development, with increasing demands for digitalization, networking, intelligence, and services in its transformation and upgrading. Additionally, with the advancements and maturity of technologies such as multi-beam antenna, frequency reuse, advanced modulation schemes, software-defined radio, software-defined payloads, software-defined networking, small satellite manufacturing, as well as technologies like multi-satellite launches and rocket reusability, the satellite industry is showing trends of miniaturization in structure, batch production, diversification in functions, and cost-effective commercialization.

Driven by the development of new technologies and diversified demands, the satellite industry is experiencing new opportunities and facing corresponding challenges. Currently, there are still shortcomings or issues in the digitalization level of certain satellite engineering systems, weak information exchange capabilities between systems, poor evolution of models and data correlation between processes, and the digitalization, networking, intelligence, and service levels of satellite products, satellite workshops, satellite networks, etc., are unable to meet diverse requirements such as rapid response, real-time control, efficient intelligence, flexible reconfiguration, and user-friendliness.At the same time, the extension of satellite networks, known as space information networks, connects satellite networks, various space vehicles, and ground broadband networks to form an intelligent system, which holds significant research significance and application prospects. The space information network has the characteristics of dynamic time-varying nodes and links, complex temporal and spatial network behavior, and huge differences in types of operation. These factors all make the establishment of such networks quite challenging, in terms of network model construction, network node management and control, dynamic networking mechanisms, and time-varying network transmission.

But it is possible to achieve satellite lifecycle management and control, as well as the construction and optimization of time-varying satellite networks and space information networks. This is accomplished by: introducing digital twin technology into the construction of space communication networks; referring to five-dimensional digital twin models to build digital twin satellites (Unit), satellite networks (System), and space information networks (System of Systems); and constructing a space information network management platform digital twin (Figure 7-2).

7.3.1.1 *Satellite digital twin*

As high-cost and complex aerospace products, satellites require smart, digital processes for design and final assembly. But currently, neither is sufficiently smart or digitized. At the same time, after satellites enter their orbits their health monitoring and maintenance also pose technical difficulties. Introducing digital twin technology into the satellite lifecycle makes it possible to realize the three applications shown in Table 7-7.

Table 7-7   Application of digital twin in the satellite lifecycle

1	Use digital twin models and simulations to assist the 3D design and verification of satellites.
2	Combine the design model with the digital twin final assembly platform to digitize the final assembly and make the process smarter.
3	Base satellite fault prediction and health management on digital twin technology. Use a sensor and operational data, combined with models and algorithms, to monitor satellites remotely, assess their conditions, predict fault occurrence, identify the cause(s) of faults, and formulate maintenance strategies.

7.3.1.2 *Satellite network digital twin*

The high-speed operation of satellite network nodes and dynamic changes among the links put forward extremely high requirements for the time-varying reconstruction of satellite network topology. Building a time-varying satellite network digital twin involves using highly realistic network models and relevant protocols and algorithms, combined with current-state data, historical data, and relevant expert knowledge databases, to establish a virtual network that mirrors the actual satellite network. The virtual network is used for high-precision simulation of network behavior and assistance in the real-time construction of satellite network topology.

7.3.1.3 *Space information network digital twin*

On the basis of time-varying satellite networking, relevant resources are integrated to build a digital twin of the space information network platform, which can monitor the status and information of the entire network in real time. Network scenarios and communication behavior are simulated using the relevant protocol models, algorithms, and simulation tools, and then the space information network is pre-configured for routing, resources are pre-allocated, and equipment is maintained beforehand for its construction and optimization.

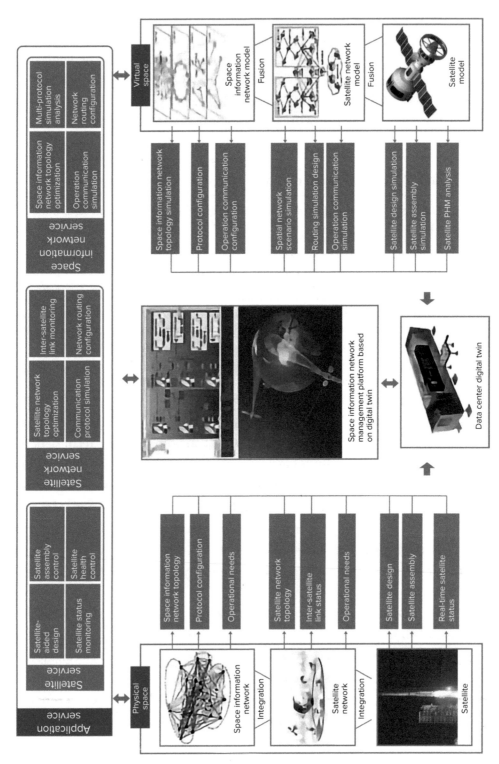

Figure 7-2 Space information network management platform digital twin

7.3.2   Shipbuilding

As the global manufacturing industry undergoes transformation and upgrading, the development of the shipbuilding industry is hampered by problems such as lagging design capabilities, insufficient digitalization of operational and maintenance control, and underdevelopment in the supporting industries. Figure 7-3 shows that an effective solution to these problems is to introduce digital twin technology to the shipbuilding industry and use the five-dimensional digital twin model to carry out the integrated management and control of the entire lifecycle of ship design, manufacturing, operation, maintenance, and usage.

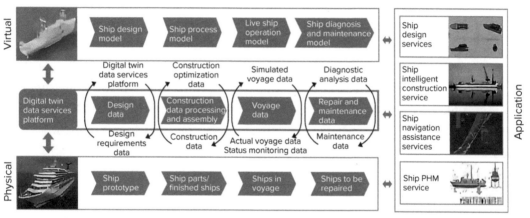

Figure 7-3 Digital twin ship lifecycle management and control model

7.3.2.1 Using digital twin to refine ship design
Currently, ship design has the shortcomings shown in Table 7-8.

Table 7-8   Shortcomings in current ship design

1	A lack of comprehensive, adequate, and effective ship lifecycle data support means that there is no effective knowledge database to aid design decisions.
2	The design model is complex, and it is difficult to unify models from various disciplines.
3	A lack of accurate simulation methods makes design verification difficult, resulting in a lengthy design phase.

In view of the above problems, digital twin technology is introduced into ship design. A large amount of ship digital twin data can support the establishment of a knowledge database and aid the relevant modeling work. Digital twin modeling technology and model fusion theory can be used to provide solutions for the construction and integration of models from various disciplines. High-fidelity digital twin simulation can improve design verification capabilities, shorten the design phase, and improve design accuracy.

7.3.2.2 Using digital twin for intelligent shipbuilding

Shipbuilding quality affects the performance, quality, development cycle, and cost of the product. At present, shipbuilding is undergoing a digital transformation, but there are still problems such as the disconnect between prototype design and process design, complicated parts management, and the lack of intuitiveness in 2D process documents. Building an intelligent shipbuilding system based on digital twin, combining digital twin ship design with process simulation, enables real-time monitoring, digital management, and process optimization. At the same time, 3D process files assist workers in their operations and stores their assembly experience and know-how in a knowledge database that can be used in subsequent process guidance and simulation training.

7.3.2.3 Using digital twin to aid ship navigation

While the cabin is a controlled environment, the outside is complex, changing, and potentially difficult to monitor during the voyage. At the same time, the navigation of large ships involves various systems on board, and there is a lack of overall digital management and control. In view of the above situation, using digital twin technology to build an auxiliary ship navigation platform allows data from the monitoring of various ship conditions to be collected and provided to the crew in real time. On the other hand, the platform can control the ship's various systems and assist with relevant optimization strategies to assist the crew with navigation work.

7.3.2.4 Using digital twin to predict faults and manage ship integrity

Safe operation and maintenance is extremely important to ships. Accurate and effective operation and maintenance methods can greatly improve the cost efficiency of predicting faults and managing the integrity of the ship.

At present, relatively inadequate work has been done on fault prediction and integrity management of ships' overall structures. It is limited by the lack of real-time data and deficiencies in theories and methods. Ship fault prediction and integrity management based on digital twin use dynamic and real-time data collection and processing to quickly capture fault phenomena and accurately identify the causes of faults, while also evaluating equipment status and performing predictive maintenance.

7.3.3 Vehicles

As our most important means of transportation, the automotive industry makes use of materials science, mechanical design, control science, and other disciplines. With so many variables, abnormalities can occur during operation in the vehicle's chassis, internal structure, parts, and functions. Different damage sources (such as collisions, dust, other external factors, etc.) will affect the vehicle to various degrees, so it is necessary to evaluate the anti-damage performance of the vehicle.

At present, physical testing is usually quite involved, a costly and inaccurate approach that does not provide much confidence. By referring to the five-dimensional digital twin model, a method for evaluating a vehicle's anti-damage performance is proposed. This method provides a comprehensive evaluation by examining the vehicle's materials, structure, parts, and functions. How this works is shown in Figure 7-4.

The evaluation of vehicle anti-damage performance based on digital twin realizes the integration and fusion of the lifecycle, elements, and operational data of physical vehicles, virtual vehicles, and services through real-time information interaction and two-way authentic mapping in order to provide reliable anti-damage evaluation services. Vehicle digital twins are composed of physical vehicles, virtual vehicles, digital twin data, dynamic real-time connections, and services. The sensing system collects damage-related data from the vehicle and transmits it to the virtual space for a highly precise simulation of the virtual vehicle. The physical and virtual data are merged to extract the anti-damage performance features of the virtual vehicle and support the construction of the model. This is a high-fidelity virtual model that contains geometric models, physical models, behavioral models, and rules models, mapping and depicting the true state of the physical vehicle. Dynamic real-time connections are powered by modern information transmission technology. Efficient, fast, and accurate detection technology enables real-time information interaction between physical vehicles, virtual vehicles, and other elements of the digital twin. Vehicle anti-damage performance evaluation integrates historical and real-time data of the vehicle for analysis, processing, and evaluation. It is also a comprehensive analysis of the vehicle's materials, structure, parts, and functions.

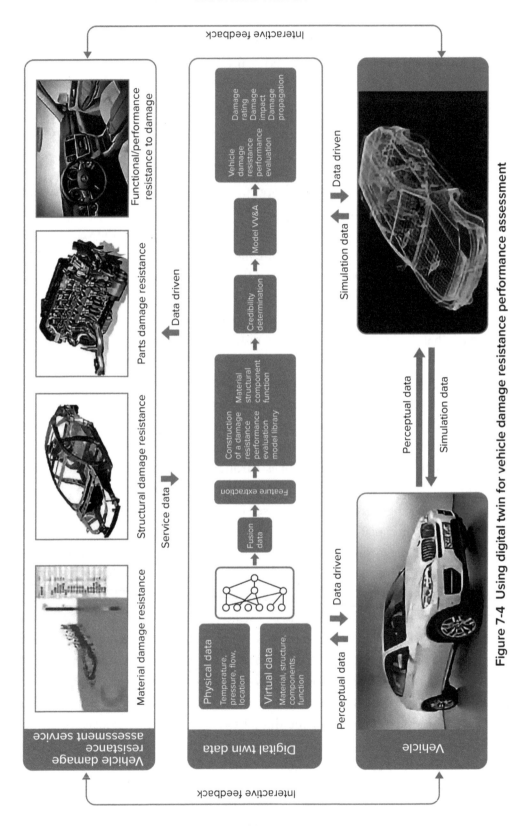

Figure 7-4 Using digital twin for vehicle damage resistance performance assessment

The digital twin vehicle can be used to accurately simulate material performance, structural changes, component integrity, and functions, so as to accurately predict and reliably evaluate the vehicle's anti-damage state, to better reflect its health and anti-damage performance.

In addition, the accumulation of relevant data can help improve the anti-damage performance of future vehicles.

7.3.4   Power plants

Thermal power generation is the main form of power generation in China. Thermal power plants operate for long periods and tend to be hot and dusty, inevitably taking a toll on the equipment.

Therefore, it is of paramount importance to ensure the normal operation of power plant equipment to guarantee that the power supply is stable and that the electrical grid is reliable and safe. In order to achieve the above goals, Beijing BKC Technology developed an intelligent, digital twin-based power plant management system (Figure 7-5). This allows for the visualization of the steam turbine generator set shaft system, so it can be monitored in real time, the visualization of rotating machinery, so they can be accurately diagnosed online, the visualization of the underground pipe network for ease of management, and 3D operational guidance.

7.3.4.1   Intelligent systems for steam turbine generator set shaft system visualization and real-time monitoring

Using real-time data, historical data, and expert knowledge of the steam turbine shaft system, a high-fidelity, 3D virtual model is built to enable observation of the inner working of the steam turbine. Using the system, the real-time status of the steam turbine can be assessed, so as to provide accurate warnings and prevent accidents such as turbine overspeeding, steam turbine shaft breakage, permanent bending of large bearings, bushing failures, and oil film instability. It also helps to optimize bearing design, valve sequencing, and operational parameters to greatly improve the operating reliability of the steam turbine generator set.

7.3.4.2   Visualization of large rotating machinery for accurate online diagnosis

The system is based on a large-scale rotating machinery virtual model and digital twin data analysis outcomes, which can remotely display equipment status, component status, problem severity, fault description, processing method, and other information in

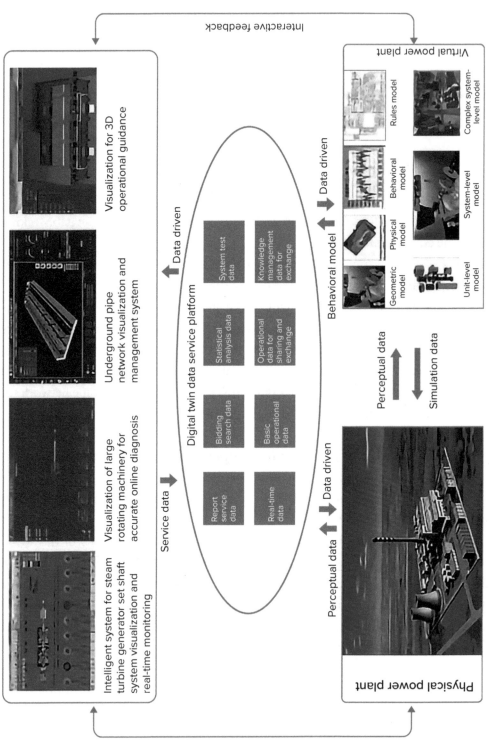

Figure 7-5 An intelligent power plant management system based on digital twin

real time and can realize remote online diagnosis of equipment. Maintenance personnel at the factory can access e-mails and webpages sent by the system to view the details of the rotating machinery through the online virtual model.

7.3.4.3 Underground pipe network visualization and management system

Laser scanning and plane design drawings are used to establish a complete and accurate 3D model of the underground pipe network. The model displays the actual location, size, and direction of all scanned components and equipment. Information on the drawings, attributes, pipeline equipment, and connector information can also be keyed in. The underground pipe network visualization system based on this model allows the pipe network to be displayed, edited, modified, and updated in 3D. Additionally, it also supports the querying, analysis, counting, and retrieval of the relevant graphics and attribute information of the underground pipe network.

7.3.4.4 Visualization for 3D operational guidance

Using real-time data, historical data, and domain knowledge of the equipment, 3D laser scanning technology can allow the creation of a complete and accurate 3D model of the equipment. The model can be used to make training courses more realistic for new employees and assist in faster learning about the equipment. It can be linked with maintenance work instructions to produce 3D work instructions for standardizing operations. It can also be used as an employee training and assessment tool.

The intelligent power plant management system based on digital twin technology enables the thorough monitoring of key equipment, precise remote fault diagnosis, visualization to aid management, precise simulation of operations, etc., for monitoring equipment condition, remote diagnosis, and maintenance. It also enables intuitive visual interaction with users.

7.3.5   Aircraft

The overall design of an aircraft is the foundation of its development. Presently, the optimization of aircraft design still faces problems such as variable coupling, data shortage, and difficulty in obtaining indicators. As an important load-bearing and controllability component of the aircraft, the landing gear bears high static and dynamic loads, with repeated usage compromising its structural integrity. How to optimize the structural design of landing gears for aircraft safety and reliability is of great significance.

A team from Beihang University partnered with Shenyang Aircraft Corporation to take the aircraft landing gear as an example. Using the five-dimensional digital twin model, the researchers explored a digital twin-based aircraft landing gear load prediction design optimization method, as shown in Figure 7-6.

During the landing and taxiing of the aircraft, both the landing gear and the fuselage of the aircraft are subjected to huge impact loads. The vertical impact load is considered to be an important factor in the fatigue damage of the landing gear. It also plays a key role in assisting and guiding the design of the landing gear. The vertical impact load is influenced by many interrelated factors. The main contributing factor forms a complex non-linear relationship with the load. Conventional modeling methods based on internal mechanism analysis are unable to build accurate models of landing gear loads. The application of digital twin technology to load forecasting is based on the establishment of a five-dimensional digital twin model of the landing gear to obtain physical data (such as equivalent mass, vertical velocity, angle of attack, etc.) virtual data (such as buffer pressure, buffer stroke, efficiency coefficient, etc.), and fusion data. Data fusion methods are then employed to forecast the load accurately, thereby predicting the impact load. The information can then be used to optimize the landing gear structure and finally achieve the goals of reducing weight, improving reliability, improving design efficiency, and reducing design costs through structural optimization. In the optimization stage of the existing design structure, the digital twin can be used to evaluate the design and form feedback for improvement. After taking into account the needs and opinions of consumers, if the landing gear is iteratively judged to not require optimization, there is no need for redesign. If there is a need to redesign the landing gear structure, then design optimization is performed. The traditional design optimization process is mainly divided into steps such as establishing target functions, determining design variables, and specifying design constraints. Based on this theory, combined with the characteristics of digital twin, virtual models are used to iteratively improve and test existing designs. If the design requirements are met, a new design is produced. Otherwise, the design optimization steps are repeated until a feasible design that meets the requirements is obtained.

After the adoption of digital twin technology a large number of experiments, tests, and calculations are carried out to simulate product design usage. Environment parameters from past tests are then integrated into the landing gear model design. In conventional landing gear design optimization, some data can only be obtained by expending a lot of manpower and material resources. Now, the digital twin model can be used for accurate and efficient calculations, which greatly simplifies the iterative design

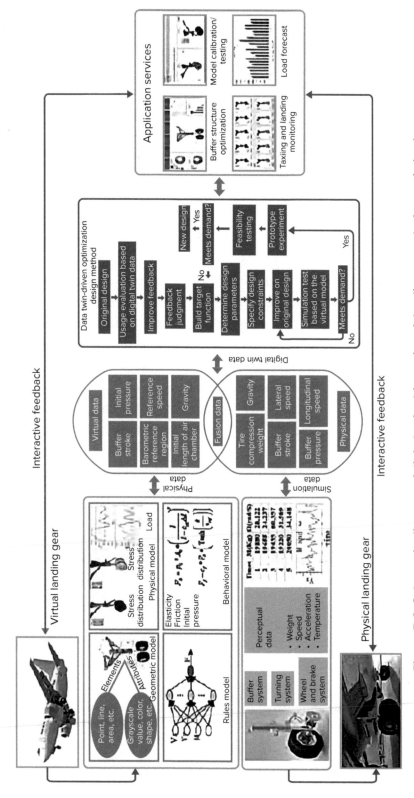

Figure 7-6 Schematic diagram of digital twin-driven aircraft landing gear design optimization

steps and improves design efficiency. After calculation and analysis, if the structural design optimization evaluation results converge, a structural design optimization plan can be generated.

7.3.6   Complex electromechanical equipment

Complex electromechanical equipment is characterized by complex structures, long operating periods, and harsh working environments.

Failure prediction, fault diagnosis, and the repair and maintenance of complex electromechanical equipment ensure their efficient, reliable, and safe operation, which is vital to the entire power system. Prognostics and health management (PHM) technology use various sensors and data processing methods to comprehensively consider and integrate equipment condition monitoring, fault prediction, maintenance decisions, etc., to extend service life and improve equipment reliability. However, PHM technology at present faces issues such as inaccurate models, incomplete data, and insufficient virtual-real interaction. The root of these problems is a lack of deep cyber-physical integration. To introduce the five-dimensional digital twin model into PHM, the model is first established and calibrated for the physical entity, and then simulations based on the model and interactive data carried out. The physical entity parameters and virtual simulation parameters are compared so that gradual and sudden failures can be predicted and identified respectively. Finally, the maintenance plan can be designed according to the cause of failures and based on dynamic simulation verification. This method has been applied to the integrity management of wind turbines, as shown in Figure 7-7.

Sensors are installed on key components such as gearboxes, motors, main shafts, bearings, etc., of the wind turbines for real-time data collection and monitoring. Based on the collected data, historical data, and domain knowledge, a multidimensional (geometric, physical, behavioral, and rules) model can be built for the virtual mapping of the actual wind turbine. Based on synchronous operation and interaction of the physical and virtual wind turbines, functions such as state detection, fault prediction, and maintenance strategy design can be realized. This is achieved through interaction and comparison of the physical and simulated states, physical and simulation data fusion and analysis, and virtual model verification. These functions can be packaged into services and provided to users in the form of application software.

The PHM method based on a five-dimensional digital twin model can use continuous virtual-real interaction, cyber-physical fusion data, and virtual model simulation verifi-

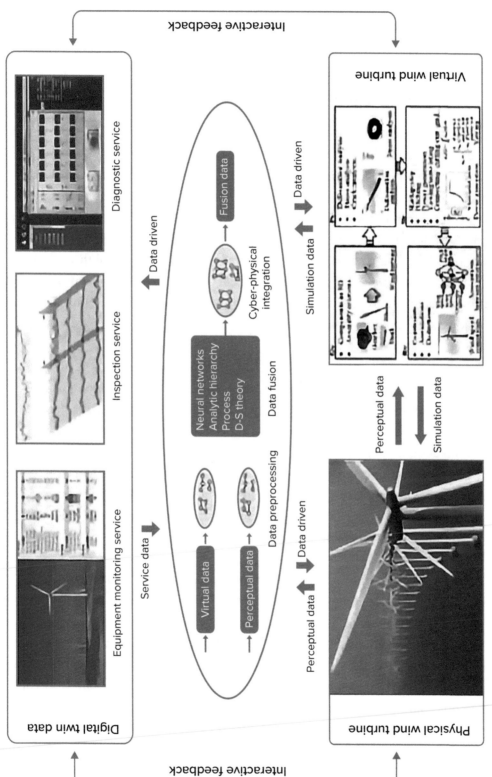

Figure 7-7 Wind turbine gearbox fault prediction based on digital twin

cation to enhance cyber-physical fusion in equipment condition monitoring and fault prediction, thereby improving the accuracy and effectiveness of the PHM method.

7.3.7 Stereoscopic warehouse

An automated stereoscopic warehouse is a kind of warehouse that uses the stacking of shelves for the efficient storage and retrieval of goods. It comprises storage shelves, storage equipment, and information management and control systems. It integrates storage technology, precise control technology, and computer information management systems. It is an important part of modern logistics systems. However, stereoscopic warehouses designed using conventional methods still face problems such as low outbound scheduling efficiency, low utilization rates, and suboptimal throughput.

As shown in Figure 7-8, the five-dimensional digital twin model can provide effective solutions for the redesign and optimization of stereoscopic warehouses, remote operations, and warehouse sharing.

7.3.7.1 Redesign and optimization of digital twin-based stereoscopic warehouses

Stereoscopic warehouse design based on digital twin technology involves the construction of five-dimensional digital twin models for each piece of equipment in the warehouse before using a design demonstration platform for hardware-in-the-loop simulation design. Using this platform, 3D graphic design of the warehouse layout can be carried out, as well as hardware-in-the-loop simulation verification based on shelves, transportation, robots, etc., providing complete geometric modeling, action script programming, and definitions for instruction interface and information interface. This enables modular packaging and model interface design customization.

7.3.7.2 Remote operation of digital twin-based stereoscopic warehouses

Using digital twin five-dimensional models of the stereoscopic warehouse and its equipment, a user-oriented service platform can be built for the remote operation of the stereoscopic warehouse. By building a virtual model that is a complete mapping of the stereoscopic warehouse and using warehouse data and information, combined with various algorithms, the real-time simulation and simulation optimization of the stereoscopic warehouse can be realized. At the same time that real-time monitoring of the status and information of the warehouse is carried out, inventory management, cargo space management, cost management, early warning management, predictive

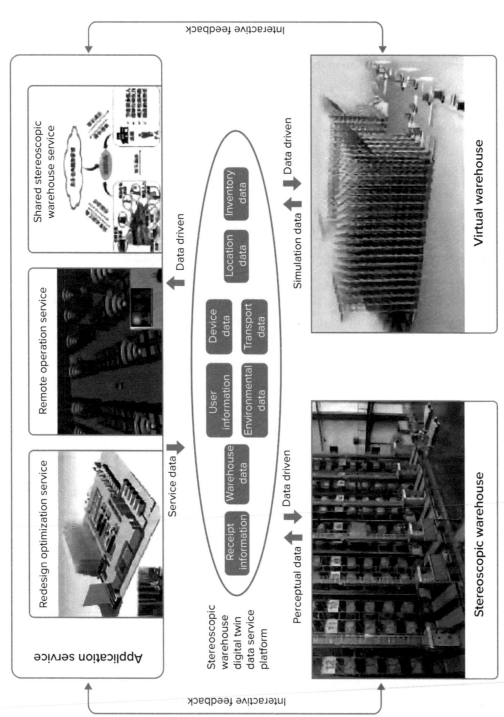

Figure 7-8 Stereoscopic warehouse based on the five-dimensional digital twin model

maintenance, job scheduling, and other functions are provided in the form of software services to users with different needs.

7.3.7.3 Sharing of digital twin-based stereoscopic warehouses

The sharing of digital twin-based stereoscopic warehouses is a new way of allocating warehousing resources optimally based on supply and demand. First, idle storage facilities, handling equipment, cargo transportation, terminal distribution, and manpower are identified and consolidated. The warehouse sharing service management cloud platform is then used for scheduling and managing the idle resources, making them accessible to companies and individuals on demand. This warehouse sharing service helps enterprises and individuals reduce their capital outlay, relieve storage pressures, and reduce investment risks.

Stereoscopic warehouse design based on digital twin allows the warehouse to be designed accurately and rapidly, saving on design costs. It is also more targeted and allows for customization. During the design process, the platform can receive data and information that are transmitted in real time, making it convenient to verify and modify the design for iterative design optimization. Through the remote operation service platform, warehouse information can be remotely dispatched and processed to improve warehouse operational efficiency. The sharing of stereoscopic warehouses maximizes the effective utilization of resources and reduces wastage and costs.

7.3.8 Healthcare

Looking back, digital twins have been primarily applied in the manufacturing industry. It started with high-end and complex manufacturing industries such as aircraft, automobiles, and ships, then expanded to industrial equipment used in these industries, electronic products in the high-tech electronics industry, and consumer products in daily life such as fashion, footwear, cosmetics, home furniture, food, and beverages. The application of digital twins is also increasing in the infrastructure industry, including railways, highways, nuclear power plants, hydropower plants, thermal power plants, urban buildings, entire cities, and even mining operations. Although digital twin systems originated in intelligent manufacturing, with the development of artificial intelligence and sensor technologies, they can also play a significant role in more complex and diverse areas such as community management. Earlier this year, Dassault Systèmes proposed expanding the digital revolution from lifeless "things" in the material world to living "life," such as managing human health and predicting diseases.

Health services include medical services, health management and promotion, health insurance, and related services. The scale of the health services industry in developed countries can reach 10% to 17% of their GDP. In contrast, in China, the health services industry is currently mainly focused on medical and health services, with a smaller scale, limited content, lagging development, and overall smaller volume in the front-end industry (disease prevention and health maintenance) and back-end industry (health promotion and enhancement).

The industry primarily focuses on elderly health services, lacking health services for chronic disease management and sub-healthy populations. Health service demands are shifting from offline models to new models where online plays a primary role and offline support, transforming from one-time medical check-ups to long-term continuous monitoring and intervention. During the pandemic, people's awareness of the lack of health services in a home setting, such as the absence of tools for continuous measurement and monitoring of personal health indicators, the lack of effective channels for residents to obtain health guidance and treatment plans from contracted family doctors efficiently, and the lack of convenient ways for residents to access high-end personalized health management services (e.g., dietary nutrition, fitness services), has increased.

Digital twins create conditions for home health services. Throughout the entire life cycle, digital twins construct digital models in virtual space that accurately map the shape, behavior, and texture of real entities in the physical space. Through visual sensors, AI chips, deep learning algorithms, and digital twin modeling technology, digital twins can monitor and provide early warnings for family members' daily activities, postures, and health risks (especially for older people). This plays a role in comprehensive care for family members' health, reducing service costs, improving the quality of home health services, reducing health risks, and achieving intelligent and refined management of family health.

In terms of specific applications of digital twin technology in the healthcare field, on the one hand, digital twins can provide real-time health monitoring and management for individuals. On the other hand, digital twins can be applied to the health systems in the medical field, providing more guidance for implementing health systems. Looking at individual health, everyone can have their digital twin in the future. By digitizing medical equipment such as surgical beds, monitors, and treatment devices and combining them with digital twins of medical assistive devices such as exoskeletons, wheelchairs, and heart stents, digital twins will become new platforms and experimental means for personal health management and healthcare services.

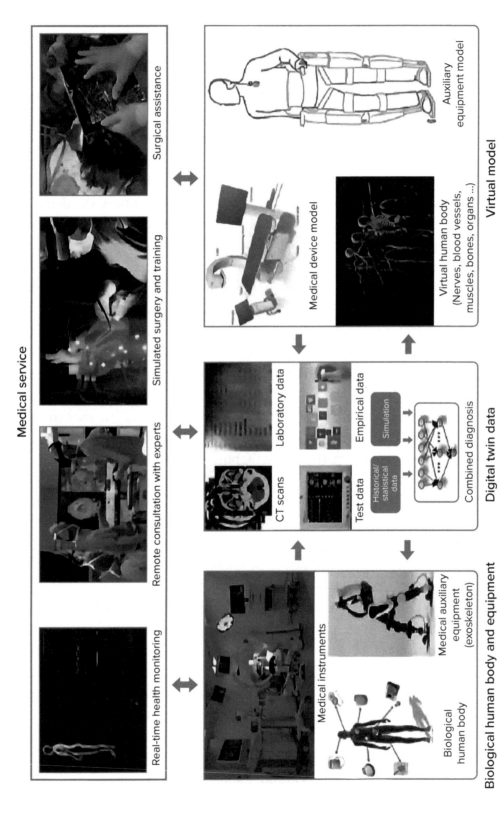

Figure 7-9 Schematic diagram of the digital twin medical system

The advancement and application of digital twin technology has made it suitable for facilitating advances in the healthcare industry. In the future, each of us will have a digital twin of our body. As shown in Figure 7-9, combining the digital twins of medical equipment (such as operating tables, monitors, treatment devices, etc.) and the digital twins of auxiliary medical equipment (such as human exoskeletons, wheelchairs, heart stents, etc.), digital twin technology will bring new platforms and methods to personal health management and medical services.

Based on the five-dimensional digital twin model, the digital twin medical system mainly comprises the following components.

7.3.8.1 *Biological human body*
Through a variety of novel medical tests, scanners, and wearable devices, both dynamic and static multiple-source human body data can be collected.

7.3.8.2 *Virtual human body*
Based on the multiscale and multidimensional data collected, the virtual human body modeled is a perfect replica. The body shape, appearance, and size of the internal organs are portrayed geometrically. The physical characteristics of nerves, blood vessels, muscles, bones, etc., are reflected. Physiological data and characteristics such as pulse and heart rate are captured. The biochemical model is the most complex, since biochemical indicators are to be displayed in the spatial scales of tissues, cells, and molecules in the order of milliseconds and microseconds.

7.3.8.3 *Digital twin data*
Medical digital twin data includes data from biological human bodies, including medical tests and scans like CT, nuclear magnetic resonance, electrocardiogram, and color Doppler ultrasound, and biochemical data, such as blood tests, urine tests, and biological enzymes. Virtual and simulation data include health forecasts, surgical simulation data, and virtual drug tests. In addition, there are historical/statistical data and medical records. These data are integrated to produce diagnoses and treatment plans.

7.3.8.4 *Medical health services*
Based on the human body digital twin, the services provided by the medical digital twin include real-time health monitoring, remote consultation with experts, virtual surgery verification and training, training for doctors, surgical assistance, drug development, etc.

7.3.8.5 *Real-time data connection*

Real-time data connection ensures the consistency of both physical and virtual components, provides comprehensive data for diagnosis and treatment, and improves diagnosis accuracy and surgical success rates.

Based on the human body digital twin, medical staff can obtain both dynamic and static data from the human body to predict the risk and probability of disease. Based on the feedback provided, users are given timely updates on their physical conditions, so they can adjust their diets and daily routines. If the user falls sick, experts in different locations are able to use the digital twin model for an online consultation to determine the cause(s) and formulate treatment plans without seeing the patient. When surgery is required, the digital twin assists in drawing up the surgical procedure before the operation; medical interns wearing head-mounted displays can then operate on the virtual human body to verify the surgical procedure, as if they were carrying out the surgery. They can carry out the surgery from multiple angles and use multiple modules to verify the feasibility of the surgical procedure and make improvements to it until they are satisfied.

Human digital twins can also be used to help medical staff train their skills and improve the success rate of operations. During the surgery, the digital twins can provide multiple perspectives and warn of risks, such as underlying bleeding hazards, so that the medical team can prepare beforehand and better cope.

In addition, pharmaceutical R&D using human digital twins, combined with molecular-or cell-level virtual simulation for experiments and clinical trials, can greatly shorten the drug development cycle. The vision for medical digital twins is to collect data from the birth of a child to form its human body digital twin, which will grow with the child and serve as its lifelong medical file and medical test subject.

7.3.9 Digital manufacturing factories

Factories are the basic units of the manufacturing industry. Digitalizing factories and making them smarter is an urgent necessity for intelligent manufacturing. With the in-depth application of IT, factories have made rapid progress in real-time data collection, IT system construction, data integration, virtual modeling, simulation, and more. On this basis, the interconnection and further integration between factory information and the physical world is the way forward and the only way for factories to achieve intelligent production and control.

The introduction of digital twin technology into the factory aims to achieve deep integration of factory information and the physical world on the basis of real-time interaction.

The digital twin factory includes the physical factory, the virtual factory, factory services, factory digital twin data, and connections. Driven by the integrated digital twin data, each part of the digital twin factory can undergo iterative operation and two-way optimization so as to optimize factory management, planning, and control.

7.3.9.1 *Digital twin factory equipment integrity management*

Managing the integrity of factory equipment mainly includes assessing equipment status based on real-time interaction and comparing physical equipment with virtual models, fault diagnosis and prediction driven by cyber-physical fusion data, and maintenance strategy design and verification based on the dynamic simulation of virtual models. Digital twin technology can be used for the timely identification of factory equipment performance degradation and the accurate location of fault causes, as well as the verification of maintenance strategies.

7.3.9.2 *Multidimensional analysis and optimization of digital twin factory energy consumption*

In terms of energy consumption analysis, the mutual calibration and fusion of cyber-physical data can improve the accuracy and completeness of energy consumption data, thereby supporting comprehensive multidimensional and multiscale analysis. In terms of energy consumption optimization, by making use of equipment parameters, process flow, and personnel behavior, the real-time simulation of virtual models can carry out iterative optimization to reduce workshop energy consumption. In terms of energy consumption assessment, the mining of digital twin data dynamically updates the rules and constraints so that multilevel and multistage dynamic analysis of actual energy consumption can be carried out.

7.3.9.3 *Digital twin factory dynamic production scheduling*

Digital twin technology can improve the reliability and effectiveness of dynamic scheduling in factories.

1) Cyber-physical fusion data is used to accurately predict the availability of equipment, thereby reducing the impact of equipment downtime on production schedules.

2) Cyber-physical interactions can pick up production disturbances (such as sudden equipment failure, emergency orders, processing time extensions, etc.) in real time so that rescheduling can be carried out in time.
3) Virtual model simulation can be used to verify the appropriateness of the scheduling strategy before its execution.

7.3.9.4 Real-time control of digital twin factory processes

Comprehensive information on the real-time status of the production process provides the data required for the virtual model to make real-time autonomous decisions. The corresponding control strategy is generated through the evaluation and prediction of the control target, which is then verified through simulation.

When there is inconsistency between actual production and its simulation, the fusion data is mined for the underlying reasons before the physical equipment is adjusted or the virtual models corrected for their synchronization and two-way optimization.

7.3.10 Smart cities

A city is an open, huge, and complex system with the characteristics of high population density, dense infrastructure, and coupling of subsystems. How to realize the real-time monitoring of its various types of data and information—and to efficiently manage its top-level design, planning, construction, operation, security, and the livelihoods of its residents—is the crux of modern city-building.

Using digital twin technology and the five-dimensional digital twin model, digital twin cities will greatly change how cities look, reshape urban infrastructure, coordinate and improve urban management decisions, ensure public order, and allow cities to function normally (Figure 7-10).

7.3.10.1 Physical city

Through the deployment of sensors in the sky, on the ground, underground, in water bodies, etc., a city's operating status can be comprehensively and dynamically monitored.

7.3.10.2 Virtual city

Through digital modeling, a virtual model corresponding to the physical city is built. The virtual city can simulate the behavior of people, events, things, traffic, the environment, etc., in the city.

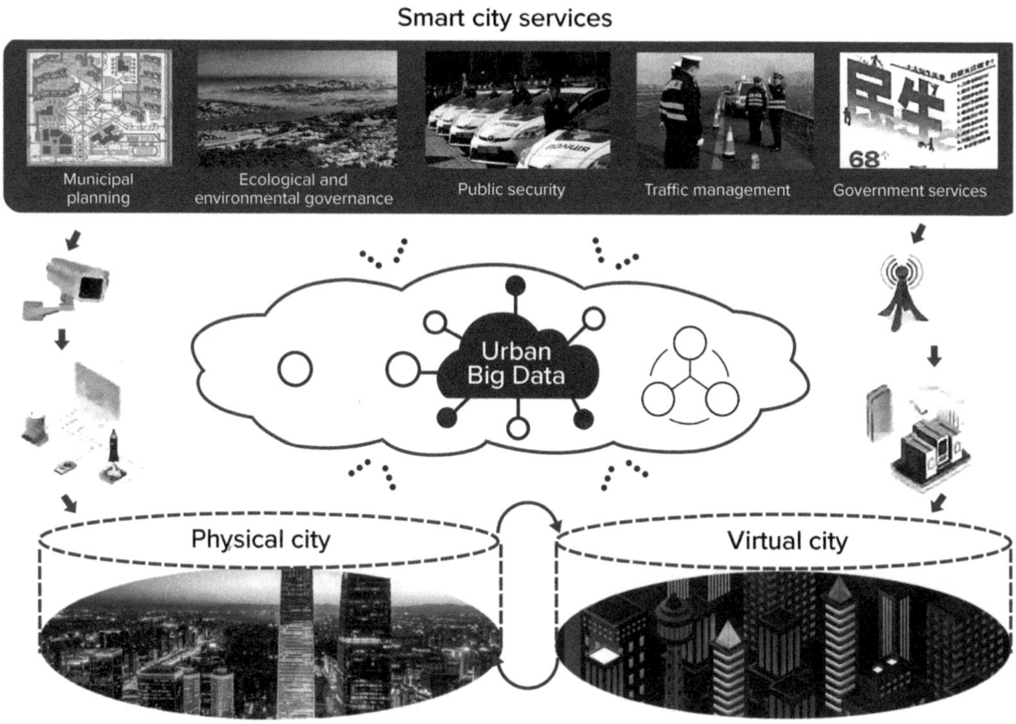

Figure 7-10 Schematic diagram of a digital twin city

7.3.10.3 Urban Big Data

This is made up of data from the urban infrastructure, transportation and environmental activities, virtual city simulations, various smart city service records, etc. It drives the development and optimization of digital twin cities.

7.3.10.4 Interaction between the virtual and the real

Expansion into the virtual space means that urban planning, construction, and various activities for residents are no longer confined to the physical world. The interaction, coordination, and integration of the physical and the virtual will define a new model of urban development for the future.

7.3.10.5 Smart services

The use of digital twins in urban planning and design guides and optimizes municipal planning, ecological and environment management, and traffic management. It also improves government services and makes urban living smarter.

The Chinese government regards digital twin cities as a necessary and effective means for the building of smart cities. In the planning outline for the Xiong'an New District in Hebei, it was clearly stated that the planning and building of the physical city and its digital twin have to be in sync so that Xiong'an can become a world-leading digital city. The China Academy of Information and Communications Technology held three successful seminars on digital twin cities to discuss their connotation, characteristics, construction, overall framework, and technical support systems. The Alibaba Cloud Research Center published the *Urban Brain Exploration "Digital Twin Cities"* white paper, proposing to build digital twin cities and use cloud computing and Big Data platforms, coupled with technologies such as the IoT and AI, to give cities "brain" functions for monitoring operational vital signs, public resource allocation, macro decision-making and command, event prediction and early warnings, etc.

In addition, notable explorations abroad include Cityzenith's 5D Smart City platform for urban management. Using this platform, the development of urban infrastructure can be digitalized and the city's lifecycle can be fully managed digitally. IBM Watson demonstrated the use of digital twin in urban buildings to control HVAC systems and monitor the indoor climate. The company also demonstrated how digital twin could be used for buildings' energy management and failure prediction and also provide technicians with service support.[32]

Digital twin technology is an effective technical means for the building of smart cities. With the help of this technology, the quality and the standards of urban planning can be improved. The technology also promotes urban design and construction and facilitates urban management and operations to make urban living and the urban environment better.

7.3.11 Smart homes

Smart homes are an inevitability in the 5G era and will be interpreted as a "cell" in a smart city (Figure 7-11). The smart home is an independent and complete individual unit. At present, the problems hindering the development of smart homes include system complexity, nonintuitive operating systems, and ineffective monitoring of the application environment and smart device usage.

As smart household appliances become more common, central management systems are needed to oversee the homes' security systems, TV networks, Wi-Fi, refrigerators, solar energy supply, water heaters, kitchen equipment, HVAC, garages, and utilities.

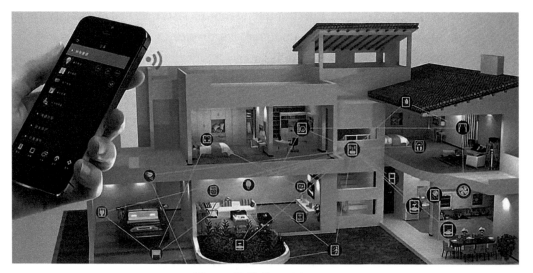

Figure 7-11 Smart homes

The current view is that the complexity of usage and management has hindered the development of the smart home industry.

With the introduction of digital twin technology, the physical living space and its accompanying equipment will be synchronously mirrored in virtual space by this technology, so that equipment operation is monitored in real time and virtual models are used for intuitive and visual interactive operation. At the same time, users can monitor and manage the household environment and equipment operation in real time. This enables better equipment maintenance to ensure reliability and comfort of use.

7.3.12 Smart logistics

In the future, smart products will be divided into two categories: physical entities and their digital twins. Product intelligence can either reside in the physical entities or their digital twins (Figure 7-12).

Between the physical entity and its digital twin, the use of reliable transmission technologies such as 5G effectively guarantees real-time updating. In the digital twin, other than just product files, there are methods of use, monitoring, control, and maintenance. Of course, more functions can be added. For the logistics industry, digital twin technology will bring significant disruptive innovation. For example, in the entire unmanned smart logistics framework, the physical entities of smart logistics objects such as shelves, handling robots, picking modules, unmanned loading systems, unmanned unloading systems, autonomous trucks, drones, and distribution robots are associated with their digital twins to build a smart logistics system control platform. Operating the digital twins through the platform enables the user to control the entire

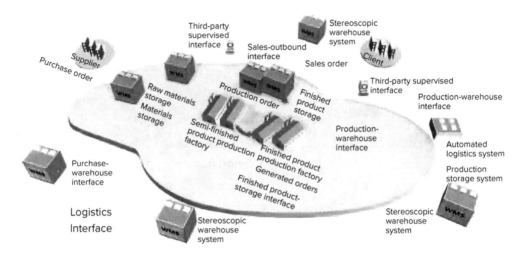

(a) Smart logistics system

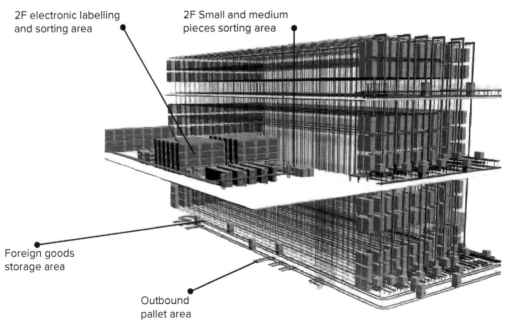

(b) Intelligent warehousing system for the manufacturing industry

Figure 7-12 Smart logistics

unmanned smart logistics system in real time. The user is also kept updated of the real-time operating status of system components and the operation of the relevant links and components to facilitate subsequent maintenance, traceability, and usage.

Digital twins are not just the digitization of items in physical logistics networks. They also include the digitization of logistics systems, operations, and equipment, and even the virtualization of goods. Digital twins synchronize virtual reality with reality in the sense that events in the physical world are reconstructed synchronously in virtual reality using digital twin technology so as to provide all parties with more convenient and intuitive management and control. In addition to real-time and intelligent control of logistics equipment, digital twin models accumulate knowledge related to smart logistics equipment, product design, and manufacturing for management and deployment, as well as improvements to design and innovation.

7.3.13   Construction

For the construction industry, especially when it comes to complex projects, digital twin technology will become a core technology that can be applied to the whole process (Figure 7-13). However, the application of digital twins in construction is somewhat

Figure 7-13 Construction industry

different from that in other fields, in that virtual buildings designed by architects are produced first so that the construction progress of the physical buildings can be monitored in real time through digital scanning. The data collected is mirrored onto digital twins for verification.

In other words, the building first exists in virtual space before real-time scanning is employed to monitor the construction methods, process, progress, etc., of the building under construction to verify whether the work is in line with the requirements and check for deviations. Digital twin technology has to be effective in preventing construction deviations and safeguarding the entire project in order to provide effective and real-time management of the construction process. Otherwise, it would be relegated to the role of post-construction review. The construction industry will be an important area for the application of digital twin technology.

7.3.14 Remote monitoring

In the future, every device in a large engineering facility or a factory will have a digital twin (i.e., the device will be mirrored and managed with the help of digital twin technology). Through digital twin technology, we can accurately understand how these physical devices operate. The seamless matching of the digital twin model and the physical device enables operating data from the equipment monitoring system to be obtained in real time for fault prediction and timely maintenance.

Monitoring is but a relatively superficial application of digital twin technology. Its real value lies in controlling and managing reality directly from virtual space.

In the future, aircraft pilots can use digital twin technology to operate physical aircraft. Through the digital models, the remote operation of equipment will become possible. Because of digital twin technology, managers will become familiar with terms like "remote assistance," "remote operation," and "remote emergency commands."

7.3.15 Personal health management

In the future, everyone will have a digital twin. From the moment a child is born, its virtual reality image will be created. Through a variety of new medical tests, scanning instruments, and wearable devices, it will be possible to produce exact digital replicas of ourselves. It will also be possible to track the operation of and changes in each part of these digital replicas, so that we can better monitor and manage our health.

Not only that but our daily food intake, the environments we come into contact with, the changes at work, and our emotional fluctuations will be recorded in our digital twins, so that doctors and medical researchers can carry out research on us, for example, to investigate the effects of the environment, food, and drugs on our physical health. Of course, this also extends to the digital twin of the human brain derived from more advanced brain-computer interface technology. The brain-computer interface will allow us to display, control, and interfere with our brain activities in real time using digital twin technology. For instance, digital twin technology can be used to diagnose and treat brain diseases more effectively.

Of course, digital twin technology can be used to realize realistic interaction in virtual space between two individuals who are physically separated. In the digital twin era, physical separation will no longer cause people to be distanced from each other.

As digital twin technology matures and becomes more common, it will be more widely applied, and digital twin technology will expand into more application fields. In the future, physical reality, virtual reality, and a reality for real-virtual interaction will co-exist. Even though most people are still somewhat unfamiliar with the technology, as it develops, it will eventually completely change how we discover, understand, and remake the world.

CHAPTER 8

DIGITAL ECONOMY INDUSTRIAL POLICY

In a discussion about digital twin, there is also a need to mention the digital economy. Digital twin is a highlight of the digital economy. So, what is the digital economy?

8.1   Defining the Digital Economy

In September 2016, the G20 Digital Economy Development and Cooperation Initiative released at the G20 Hangzhou summit pointed out that in a digital economy, digital knowledge and information are key production factors, while modern information networks form an important medium, and infocommunication technology is used effectively to improve efficiency and optimize the economic structure.

Depending on the degree of digitalization, the "digital" in the digital economy can refer to three different phases: information digitization, operation digitalization, and digital transformation. Digital transformation is a new phase in digital development. In this phase, digitalization not only expands the space for new economic development and promotes sustainable economic development, but also promotes the transformation and upgrading of traditional industries and brings about the transformation and development of society.

In the wake of the agricultural and industrial economies, the digital economy is a new economic form, an outcome of the IT revolution. It injects new vigor into the economy; it is innovative, green, open, and promotes sharing. As a new economic form, the digital economy has become the main source of economic growth and an important driving force for transformation and upgrading. At the same time, it is also a new high ground that global industrial players are competing for.

On April 18, 2019, the Digital Economy Development and Employment in China white paper published by the China Academy of Information and Communications Technology showed that the scale of China's digital economy reached RMB 31.3 trillion in 2018, a year-on-year increase of 20.9%, accounting for 34.8% of the country's GDP. Industrial digitalization has become the main engine of digital economic growth. In recent years, the growth rate and volume of the digital economy have attracted much attention. The reason is that the speed at which the digital economy is developing is significantly higher than that of traditional economic sectors. At the same time, because the digital economy has become an important driver in changing the trajectory and accelerating some local economic development, the scale, proportion, and growth rate of the digital economy in Chinese provinces and cities have become the focus of attention.

8.2 Digital Economy Strategies and Industrial Policies of Major Countries and Regions around the World

A growing number of countries are now aware of the strategic role that the digital economy plays in national development and have formulated relevant strategies and policies to ensure and promote healthy and long-term development of their digital economies in tandem with technological development.

8.2.1 The United States—putting America first to consolidate the dominant position of its digital economy

In 2018, the United States rolled out the Strategic Plan for Data Science (Table 8-1), Strategy for American Leadership in Advanced Manufacturing (Table 8-2), etc., to articulate its plans to promote the development of its digital economy.

Table 8-1   Strategic Plan for Data Science

Overview
Publication date: June 4, 2018 Policy name: Strategic Plan for Data Science Issuing agency: National Institutes of Health
Policy aim
New technologies such as machine learning and VR are used to manage the large volume of national biomedical research data, and a roadmap for promoting the modernization of biomedical data science management is laid out.
Policy content
1. Support the construction of efficient and safe biomedical research data infrastructure. Optimize data storage, improve data security, and connect different data systems.
2. Promote the modernization of the data ecosystem. Support the storage and sharing of personal data, and integrate clinical and scientific data into biomedical data science.
3. Promote the development and use of advanced data management, analytical, and visualization tools. Support the development of practical and universal tools and workflows that are barrier-free.
4. Enhance the cultivation of teams of biomedical data science talents and formulate corresponding policies to promote the sustainable development of data science management.

Table 8-2   Strategy for American Leadership in Advanced Manufacturing

Overview
Publication date: October 5, 2018 Policy name: Strategy for American Leadership in Advanced Manufacturing Issuing agency: The White House
Policy aim
This policy discloses for the first time the U.S. government's strategic plan to ensure that the U.S. will occupy a leading position in the advanced manufacturing industry in the future. It aims to expand manufacturing employment, support the development of the manufacturing industry, and ensure a strong foundation for the defense industry and a controllable, flexible supply chain through the development plans. It also aims to help the country achieve global leadership in advanced manufacturing across fields to bolster national security and safeguard economic prosperity.

(Continued)

Main content	*Digital economy-related matters*
1. Sort out the factors that affect innovation and competitiveness in advanced manufacturing, focusing on the trend of close integration between manufacturing, technological development, and market orientation; manufacturing technology development and infrastructure building; a reliable intellectual property legal system; trade policies that are conducive for manufacturing; science, technology, engineering and mathematics education of high standards; and an industrial foundation for manufacturing. 2. Put forward three core goals to ensure the leading position of its advanced the manufacturing industry, namely the development and application of new manufacturing technologies; education, training, and agglomeration of manufacturing labor; and expansion of its domestic manufacturing supply chain capabilities. For each core goal, several strategic goals and corresponding series of specific priorities have been determined. For each strategic task, the main federal government agencies responsible for implementation have also been designated. 3. Emphasize the need for strong support to key areas that guide the development of the global manufacturing industry. Promote the transfer and transformation of fundamental research to scientific research outcomes. Strive for continuous technological innovation and industrial application in key areas.	Based on the strategic goal of "Capture the future of intelligent manufacturing systems," four specific priorities were proposed: 1. Smart and digital manufacturing. Use Big Data analytics and advanced sensing and control technologies to promote the digital transformation of the manufacturing industry, and use real-time modeling, simulation, and data analysis of products and processes to develop common standards for intelligent manufacturing. 2. Advanced industrial robotics. Promote the development of new technologies and standards for the wider adoption of robotics, and promote safe and effective human-computer interaction. 3. AI infrastructure. Develop new standards for AI and identify the best practices to provide consistent manufacturing data, while maintaining data security and respecting intellectual property rights. Prioritize development of new approaches to data access, confidentiality, encryption, and risk assessment for US manufacturers. 4. Cybersecurity in manufacturing. Develop standards, tools, and testbeds, and disseminate guidelines for implementing cybersecurity in smart manufacturing systems.

8.2.2 Germany—formulating a strategy for high technology and enhancing AI strategy implementation

In 2018, Germany rolled out the AI Made in Germany (Table 8-3) and High-Tech Strategy 2025 (Table 8-4) policies, making it clear that it is promoting the application of AI.

Table 8-3   AI Made in Germany

Overview
Publication date: November 15, 2018 Policy name: AI Made in Germany Issuing agency: German Federal Government
Policy aim
The policy aims to make AI a national priority and proposes an overall framework for its development and application. Three billion euros will be invested for the implementation of this policy by 2025 to close the AI software and innovation gap between Germany and the United States and Asia.
Policy content
The policy comprehensively considers the impact of AI on all areas of society, quantitatively analyzes the economic benefits that AI can bring to the manufacturing industry, emphasizes the use of AI to serve small- and medium-sized enterprises and pays particular attention to the potential impact of AI on social policies and labor. At the same time, five breakthrough areas are proposed, namely: machine-based proofs and deduction systems, knowledge-based systems, pattern recognition and analysis, robotics, and smart multi-modal human-computer interaction.
Main measures
1. Use AI to enhance Germany's competitiveness. Establish a national innovation network composed of 12 AI research centers. Plan and build AI innovation clusters in Europe. Support start-ups and small-/medium-sized enterprises with digital technology and business models. 2. Use AI to benefit the public, environment, and climate. Initiate 50 flagship applications in the areas of environment and climate. 3. Pay attention to data protection laws and systems. Join hands with data protection regulatory agencies and business associations to formulate guidelines and relevant legislation for the application of AI systems so as to protect data belonging to individuals and enterprises.

Table 8-4   High-Tech Strategy 2025

Overview
Publication date: September 5, 2018 Policy name: High-Tech Strategy 2025 Issuing agency: German Federal Cabinet

(Continued)

Policy aim
This policy provides the strategic framework for Germany's high-tech development. It clarifies the cross-departmental tasks, landmark goals, and key areas of Germany's research and innovation policy for the next seven years. With the theme of "Research and Innovation for the People," research and innovation will ensure that the country continues to develop and prosper. Sustainable development and rising living standards will go hand in hand. Fifteen billion euros will be invested to implement this policy with the aim of promoting technological research and innovation in Germany to cope with future challenges, improve quality of life for Germans, and consolidate the country's position as an innovation powerhouse.

Main content	Digital economy-related matters
1. Respond to major social challenges, including fighting cancer, developing intelligent medicine, drastically reducing plastic discharge into the environment, launching an industrial decarbonization plan, developing a sustainable circular economy, protecting biodiversity, developing networked driving, and promoting battery research. 2. Strengthen Germany's future high-tech capabilities. Develop microelectronics, communication systems, materials, quantum technology, modern life sciences, and aerospace research, and strengthen Germany's future high-tech capabilities through the three areas of key technologies, professional talents, and societal participation. 3. Establish an open innovation and venture culture. Support the development of an open innovation and venture culture, provide space for creative ideas, attract new participants in innovation, promote knowledge transfer, enhance the entrepreneurial and innovation capabilities of small-and medium-sized enterprises, and deepen the innovation partnership between Germany, Europe, and other regions in the world.	In the area of "Strengthening Germany's future competencies," the application of AI will be promoted and the national AI strategy will be used to bolster Germany's capabilities in this area. 1. Promote capacity building in machine learning, promote the use of learning systems, develop new methods of Big Data editing and analysis and generate knowledge and create value from data. 2. Establish AI professorships in universities, expand the professional talent base, and greatly increase the industrial usage of AI to stimulate entrepreneurial activity. 3. Intensify the discourse with society regarding fields of technology such as AI, the application of Big Data methods, and the interaction between humans and technology. Set up a Data Ethics Commission to propose a development framework for data policy, the handling of AI, and digital innovation.

8.2.3   Japan—focusing on technological solutions and committing to the Society 5.0 plan

In 2018, Japan published the White Paper on Manufacturing Industries (Table 8-5), the second Strategic Innovation Promotion Program (SIP) (Table 8-6), etc., detailing its action plan for driving the development of its digital economy.

Table 8-5   White Paper on Manufacturing Industries in Japan

Overview	
Publication date: June 14, 2018 Policy name: White Paper on Manufacturing Industries in Japan Issuing agency: Ministry of Economy, Trade and Industry	
Policy aim	
Since 2002, the Japanese government started publishing its annual White Paper on Manufacturing Industries in May or June, with the aim of analyzing and solving the problem of persistently low yields faced by the Japanese manufacturing industry. According to the document, the global manufacturing industry is currently in a stage of discontinuous innovation. The white paper also identifies the development of interconnected industries as a strategic goal in the development of its manufacturing industry.	
Main content	*Digital economy-related matters*
1. Analysis of the current state of the Japanese manufacturing industry. Emphasizes the importance of "field force" in raising productivity and promotes the development of interconnected industries. Highlights the need for more effective manufacturing training, building a universal ability evaluation system, and cultivating teaching and manufacturing talents for a super-smart society. 2. Summary of the basic technology promotion measures of the manufacturing industry in 2017 and evaluation of the progress of basic technology R&D measures in the manufacturing industry, including the acquisition and use of intellectual property rights, the standardization and certification of technologies, the training of tech and innovation talents, and the application and transformation of research outcomes.	1. Proposed the use of digital tools to enhance "field force" in manufacturing, namely the use of robotics, IoT, and AI to achieve automation, increase productivity, and cope with manpower shortages. 2. Made it clear that the future lay with interconnected industries. Proposed the use of digital tools such as the IoT, Big Data, and AI flexibly to connect people, equipment, systems, and technologies, to produce solutions that integrate automation and digitalization, and to create new added value.

(Continued)

3. In manufacturing, promote the development of industrial clusters, innovation and entrepreneurship by small and medium enterprises, and strategic sectors. 4. Promote the learning of basic manufacturing technologies. Enhance manufacturing training in schools and promote lifelong learning related to manufacturing.	3. Proposed the development of strategic industrial sectors such as robotics and autonomous driving, along with improved infrastructural support for these sectors. Emphasized the importance of network security in these sectors.

Table 8-6   2nd Strategic Innovation Promotion Program (SIP)

Overview	
Publication date: July 31, 2018 Policy name: 2nd Strategic Innovation Promotion Program (SIP) Issuing agency: Council for Science, Technology and Innovation	
Policy aim	
The policy aims to promote the transformation of basic technology research outcomes into practical applications, solve important livelihood problems, boost the Japanese economy, and improve the country's comprehensive industrial capabilities. It also aims to promote technology R&D, achieve technological innovation, and build a super-smart Society 5.0.	
Main content	*Digital economy-related matters*
1. Use basic cyberspace technology based on Big Data and AI to achieve a high degree of collaboration between machines and humans, as well as cross-domain data collaboration.	1. Use basic cyberspace technology based on Big Data and AI to develop the base technology for human-computer interaction and achieve a high level of collaboration between machines and humans. Carry out prototype design and effectiveness verification in various fields (nursing, education, reception, etc.). Promote cross-domain data collaboration infrastructure construction, while developing the base technology for cooperation between artificial intelligence.

(Continued)

2. Develop physical space digital data processing technology, develop universal platform technology for realizing IoT solutions, and implement social applications for Society 5.0.

3. Establish cyber-physical security that corresponds to an IoT society, establish and maintain a chain of trust, and ensure the security of IoT systems, services, and supply chains.

4. Expand autonomous driving systems and services.

5. Revolutionize the integrated materials development system, and develop the base technology and application of the material integration inverse problem.

6. Ride on Society 5.0 to develop laser processing, optical quantum communication, and optoelectronic information technology.

7. Develop base technologies to make the life sciences and agricultural industries smarter. Set up an intelligent food chain and a new sanitation system.

8. Implement an energy system for a carbon-free society, develop technologies related to energy management and a wireless power transmission systems, and develop innovative technologies for high carbon resource utilization.

9. Enhance national resilience (disaster prevention and mitigation), develop a comprehensive support system for evacuation and emergency activities, and implement an integrated municipal disaster response system.

10. Develop an advanced hospital diagnosis and treatment system driven by AI.

11. Promote the development of smart logistics.

12. Innovate in deep sea resource research technology, study the reserves of resources like rare earth mud and other marine minerals, and develop deep sea resource survey and production technology.

2. Expand autonomous driving systems and services. Promote the development and verification of autonomous driving systems, develop signal information providing technologies, develop basic technologies for the practical usage of autonomous driving, and work on the social acceptance of autonomous driving technologies.

3. Develop intelligent life science industry and base agricultural technology. Establish an intelligent food chain, and combine Big Data and biotechnology to carry out data-driven breeding.

4. Establish AI hospitals with advanced diagnosis and treatment systems. Develop a highly secure medical information database, as well as medical information selection and analysis technology. Use AI to automatically record various administered medical treatments, and develop AI diagnosis, monitoring, and treatment technology that is able to utilize patients' physiological information.

5. Expand smart logistics systems. Build a logistics and commercial flow data platform, and develop visualization technology for object movement and product information.

8.2.4 Russia—emphasizing new scientific and technological development, becoming a world-class science education center

In 2018, the Presidential Address to the Federal Assembly (Table 8-7) and the Executive Order On National Goals and Strategic Objectives of the Russian Federation through to 2024 (Table 8-8) highlighted the need for Russia to promote the development of its digital economy and related fields.

Table 8-7 Presidential Address to the Federal Assembly

Overview
Publication date: March 1, 2018 Policy name: Presidential Address to the Federal Assembly Issuing agency: The President of Russia

Policy aim
The Address elaborates Russia's development strategy in the fields of science and technology. Since the adoption of its Constitution in 1993, it has become an annual practice for the Russian President to address the Federal Assembly. Although the address does not have a direct legal effect, it plays a significant role in guiding Russia's vision for strategic development.

Main content	*Digital economy-related matters*
1. The well-being of citizens is a major factor in national development. Reform the employment system to increase the employment rate and ensure the growth of national pensions. Continue to promote sustainable population growth. 2. Formulate and implement national development programs for cities and other residential areas. Urban development should become a driving force for national development and enhancing modern infrastructure. 3. Improve the living conditions of citizens. Increase national income, lower mortgage loan interest rates, and increase the housing market supply.	1. Develop a progressive legal framework as soon as possible to provide a legal basis for the development and application of cutting-edge technologies such as robotics, AI, unmanned driving, and Big Data. 2. Establish a national digital platform compatible with the global information space to provide data services for restructuring manufacturing processes, finance, and logistics. 3. Build 5G data transmission networks and IoT connections.

(Continued)

4. Develop modern transportation. Standardize regional and local roads, develop Eurasian transport arteries and inter-regional route systems, and increase railway transport capacity. 5. Develop modern medical services. Promote the establishment of an effective healthcare system and establish a unified data platform for the national healthcare system. 6. Ensure high standards of ecological balance and well-being. Enhance the environmental conservation requirements on enterprises and improve the quality of drinking water. 7. Improve cultural standards for the people. 8. Enhance the education and training of young people. 9. Promote the development of science and technology. 10. Develop a digital public administration system. Ensure that all public services can be provided in real time remotely within six years, and digitize the circulation of government documents. 11. Build the latest strategic weapon systems, and actively develop advanced technologies and new strategic weapons.	4. Build on the excellence of the national mathematics school and establish international centers for mathematics, so that Russia has a greater competitive advantage in the digital economy era.

Table 8-8   Executive Order on National Goals and Strategic Objectives of the Russian Federation through to 2024

Overview
Publication date: May 7, 2018 Policy name: Executive Order on National Goals and Strategic Objectives of the Russian Federation through to 2024 Issuing agency: The President of Russia
Policy aim
The Executive Order laid out Russia's six-year development blueprint, determined Russia's national development goals and strategic tasks in the social, economic, educational, and scientific fields to be achieved by 2024, and clearly stated Russia's aim to become top five in the world in priority technological development areas like intelligent manufacturing, robotic systems, and intelligent transportation systems by 2024.

(Continued)

195

Main content	Digital economy-related matters
1. Proposed twelve priority development areas and specific action goals. Priority development areas include population, health, education, housing and the urban environment, ecological environment, public transportation infrastructure, labor and employment, science, the digital economy, culture, small and medium enterprises, and international cooperation. 2. Put forward nine major national development goals: sustainable population growth, longer life expectancy, steady increase in real income, halving the national poverty rate, improved living conditions for Russian families, accelerated technological development, the introduction of digital technology into society and the economy, stable economic growth, and the creation of basic sectors of the economy based on emerging technologies.	1. Establish a legal supervision system for the digital economy. 2. Build digital infrastructure that is internationally competitive. Realize the high-speed transmission, processing, and storage of massive amounts of data. 3. Cultivate high-quality digital economy talents. 4. Develop information security technology. Ensure data security for individuals, businesses, and the country. 5. Develop "end-to-end" digital technology. 6. Introduce digital technology and platform solutions into public services, health, education, industry, and other fields. 7. Support the application of and R&D investment in digital technology and platform solutions. Carry out digital upgrades in priority sectors such as health, education, industry, agriculture, transportation, energy infrastructure, and finance. Provide various financing channels for the development of digitalization technologies. 8. Formulate a digital economy development plan.

8.2.5   South Korea—system reform and technological innovation

In 2018, South Korea rolled out the 4th Science and Technology Basic Plan (2018–2022) (Table 8-9) and the Innovative Growth Engine five-year plan (Table 8-10) to highlight the priority measures taken to promote digital economy development.

Table 8-9   4th Science and Technology Basic Plan (2018–2022)

Overview
Publication date: February 2018 Policy name: 4th Science and Technology Basic Plan (2018–2022) Issuing agency: South Korean government

(Continued)

196

Policy aim	
This is South Korea's fourth science and technology five-year plan and is the highest-level plan in the field in South Korea. It focuses on using "science and technology to change the lives of South Koreans." With talent at its core and by rolling out the science and technology 2040 blueprint, it links the long-term vision to the basic plan in order to produce an important strategy for the development of science and technology in the next five years.	

Main content	Digital economy-related matters
1. Establish a new R&D system centered on researchers and cultivate researchers' innovation and integration skills. 2. Establish a technological ecosystem for integration and innovation. Integrate technology into all economic and social sectors. Strengthen cooperation between industry and academia. 3. Use science and technology to cultivate emerging industries and create good employment opportunities. Establish a network foundation for real-time connection and management of people, objects, and information. Promote industrial development through innovative growth engines. 4. Use technology to improve living standards for South Koreans and solve global environmental and energy issues.	1. Included AI, smart cities, and 3D printing in the plan's 120 key technology projects for the first time. 2. Highlighted the need to continue developing AI and blockchain technology. 3. Proposed Big Data, next-generation communications, AI, autonomous vehicles, unmanned aerial vehicles, smart cities, VR/AR, customized healthcare, smart robots, smart semiconductors, etc., as innovative growth engine technologies that the government should focus on developing, so as to promote economic development and lead the fourth industrial revolution.

Table 8-10   Innovative Growth Engine Five-Year Plan

Overview	
Publication date: April 6, 2018 Policy name: Innovative Growth Engine Five-Year Plan Issuing agency: Ministry of Science and ICT	
Policy aim	
The policy aims to foster new industries based on R&D and accelerate economic development through innovative growth engines. It was stated in the plan that growth engines will change South Korea by 2022, and the country should use them to prepare for the fourth industrial revolution. The policy also outlined four major innovation growth engines and 12 technological directions.	

(Continued)

Main content	Digital economy-related matters
1. Develop smart infrastructure. Technological directions include Big Data, 5G, commercialization of the IoT and AI. 2. Develop the field of intelligent mobile objects. Technological directions include autonomous vehicles and unmanned aerial vehicles. 3. Develop the field of convergence services. Technological directions include smart cities, VR and AR, customized healthcare, and intelligent robots. 4. Develop the industrial base. Technological directions include novel drugs, new and renewable energy sources, smart semiconductors, and advanced materials.	1. Improve the accuracy of Big Data predictive analysis, use 5G commercialization and IoT hyperlink services to kickstart and promote convergence services, and overcome technological gaps through the development and promotion of core AI technologies. 2. Achieve Level 3 autonomous vehicles and construction of autonomous transport systems. Develop and commercialize drone technology for the public and companies. 3. Improve VR/AR fusion content/service/platform/equipment and other related technologies, develop personalized healthcare and precision medicine systems, and develop and upgrade intelligent manufacturing robots and medical safety service robots. 4. The plan is to acquire the core technology for AI semiconductors by 2022.

8.3 An Analysis of the Key Points in Digital Economy Industry Support Policies of Various Regions in China

Developing the digital economy has become an important starting point for China to utilize Big Data and promote high-quality economic development. The digital economy has played a leading role in stabilizing growth, advancing structural adjustments, and promoting transformation. At present, the overall framework for China's digital economy is basically in place, and the formation of the specific policy system will gather momentum. Among them, the Internet Plus high-quality development policy system is being impended. A series of major Internet Plus and digital economy projects may follow.

Both central and local governments are planning new digital economy policies, with the establishment of a digital economy policy system now a top priority. It is understood that this policy system may include policies for promoting the overall development of the digital economy, regulatory or governance policies, related environmental policies, and policies related to the development of industries important to the digital economy, such as Big Data, AI, and cloud computing.

In February 2016, Guizhou Province issued the first provincial-level digital economy plan in China.

The Guangxi Zhuang Autonomous Region, Anhui Province, and other areas have also introduced policy measures to support the development of the digital economy, focusing on things such as Big Data and AI. Within provinces like Shandong and Jiangxi, growth targets have been set for the digital economy to account for more than 30% of GDP, and the upgrading of traditional industries, along with the construction of 5G and other IT infrastructure elements will be used to reach those goals. For example, the 2019–2023 Tianjin City Action Plan for Promoting Digital Economy Development announced on June 3, 2019, stated the city's aim to lead the country in terms of the digital economy as a percentage of its GDP by 2023. To this end, it needs to build intelligent IT infrastructure, provide full fiberoptic network coverage in the city center, and accelerate the construction of 5G infrastructure.

Zhejiang Province aims to earn RMB 400 billion in revenue from 5G-related industries by 2022 and RMB 2.5 trillion in revenue from core industries that support the digital economy.

Beijing indicated that it will accelerate industrialization projects such as the smart manufacturing of 5G communication equipment and intelligent operating systems for equipment to promote the rapid digital economy development.

The following are some support policies formulated in recent years in various regions to promote the development of the Chinese digital economy. Digital economy industrial policies like the 2017–2020 Guizhou Province Digital Economy Development Plan, Fujian Province Digital Economy Development Project Special Fund Management Measures, Several Policies on Supporting Digital Economy Development by Anhui Province, and Implementation Details for Several Policies to Support Digital Economy Development by Anhui Province were analyzed, with a focus on the following six aspects:

1) Digital transformation and application showcase
2) Building innovative and service-oriented platforms
3) Building a digital economy ecosystem
4) Cultivating key market entities
5) Motivating talent and establishing academic disciplines
6) Enhancing key resources and support

8.3.1 Comparison and analysis of provinces, autonomous regions, and municipalities with policies that focus on digital transformation and application showcase

Table 8-11 Comparison and analysis of provinces, autonomous regions, and municipalities with policies that focus on digital transformation and application showcase

	Digital transformation	*Encouraging enterprises to use cloud services*
Hunan		
Tianjin		
Fujian		Support digital Fujian technical support units in centralizing their purchase of cloud computing and other digital economy infrastructure and public platform services. Support provincial departments and units in developing informatization applications and services through purchasing services.
Guangxi	For enterprises that invest RMB 20 million or more in fixed assets (i.e., plants and equipment), smart technologies, and Industrial Internet transformation in a year, 5% of the annual fixed asset investment will be subsidized, up to a maximum of RMB 5 million. For key industrialization and informatization integration projects, those that perform well will be given subsidies of up to 5% of their investment in IT software and hardware for the past three years, up to a maximum of RMB 1 million per project. A one-time award of RMB 100,000 will be given to enterprises that are included in the pilot implementation of the Ministry of Industry and Information Technology's industrialization and informatization integration management system.	Implement a "cloud service coupon" financial subsidy system. Establish a joint incentive mechanism amongst companies looking to utilize cloud services, cloud service providers, and all levels of government finance departments. Encourage cloud service providers to provide discounts, introduce financial subsidy ratios and caps at all levels in the region, use government funds to subsidize the purchase of cloud services by enterprises registered in the region, and issue "cloud service coupons" to local enterprises to make it cheaper for them to purchase cloud services.

(Continued)

	Digital transformation	Encouraging enterprises to use cloud services
Guizhou		Provide vouchers to encourage companies to make use of cloud services. Eligible companies can apply for and utilize the vouchers to defray part of the usage fee when purchasing cloud services. Each company can apply for a maximum of RMB 50,000 in coupons per year; 40% of the amount applied for can be spent on IaaS cloud services and the remaining 60% on PaaS and SaaS cloud services.
	Establishing an application demonstration benchmark	Promoting new models such as purchasing services
Hunan		Select a few mobile Internet and Big Data platforms/products with strong market demand and technical superiority, and accelerate their usage in social management and public service within the province. Explore the adoption of a public private partnership (PPP) model to promote the utilization of mobile Internet and Big Data platforms/products.
Tianjin	Develop a batch of pilot demonstration projects for Big Data, new cybersecurity, and informatization technologies, new products, new models, etc. Award enterprises with approved national-level Big Data or cyberspace pilot demonstration projects up to RMB 5 million. For key projects in the core industries of Big Data, cybersecurity, and informatization, up to 20% of the actual investment amount will be provided as financial support, capped at RMB 5 million.	

(Continued)

	Establishing an application demonstration benchmark	*Promoting new models such as purchasing services*
Fujian	Support the development of regional and industry-specific digital economy pilot demonstrations. Support the development of innovative applications for new technologies (e.g. the Internet, IoT, and satellite applications), business formats, and business models. Provide subsidies of up to RMB 3 million for application demonstration projects.	For Internet companies purchasing data center services from key digital economy industrial parks, such as the Digital Fujian (Changle) Industrial Park and the Digital Fujian (Anxi) Industrial Park, up to 30% of the resulting annual cost incurred by each company will be subsidized, with the annual subsidy for each company capped at RMB 300,000.
Guangxi		
Guizhou		Encourage greater participation in the development of public services. Encourage cooperation between the government, companies, and social organizations. Increase government procurement of products and services in cloud computing, Big Data, etc. Rely on professionals to develop government data applications, and use public sector demand to grow the market demand for the digital economy.

8.3.2 Comparison and analysis of provinces, autonomous regions, and municipalities that focus on the development of innovative service-oriented platforms

Table 8-12 Comparison and analysis of provinces, autonomous regions, and municipalities that focus on the development of innovative service-oriented platforms

	Supporting innovative public service platforms	Supporting the development of cloud services and other platforms
Anhui		Encourage companies to make breakthroughs in key technologies such as data integration, platform management, development tools, microservice frameworks, modeling, and analysis. The building of Industrial Internet (cloud) platforms is also encouraged. A number of enterprise-level Industrial Internet (cloud) platforms will be selected each year and rewarded with a bonus of RMB 500,000 each. Similarly, a number of Industrial Internet (cloud) public platforms will be selected each year and rewarded with a bonus of RMB 1 million each. Establish a dynamically managed Industrial Internet (cloud) service resource catalogue. Recognize and commend the efforts of outstanding service providers.
Hunan	Encourage industrial parks, enterprises, and social organizations to build public resource platforms such as application testing platforms, cloud services platforms, data centers, and industry public technical services platforms, and subsequently continue to improve platform support functions. Provincial authorities will provide subsidies not exceeding 20% of the platform construction cost, capped at RMB 10 million. This is done to make the public service system more professional, networked, and integrated.	

(Continued)

	Supporting innovative public service platforms	Supporting the development of cloud services and other platforms
Tianjin		
Fujian	An investment subsidy of no more than RMB 5 million will be given for investments in digital economy innovation platforms and key industries' public platforms by enterprises and institutions (including universities and scientific research institutions).	
Guangxi		The autonomous region supports leading companies in industries to invest in the building of public service cloud platforms and shared economy platforms. Following verification, these projects will be subsidized using the relevant service industry special funds. The amount of subsidy is capped at 10% of the actual outlay on the project, and the actual subsidy for a single project shall not exceed RMB 15 million.
Guizhou	Promote the integration of Big Data industry elements, support and encourage enterprises to develop Big Data industry public R&D technology service platforms. For investments of more than RMB 10 million in specialized public R&D technology service platforms, a one-time incentive of 10% of the investment amount, capped at RMB 10 million, will be granted after verification by the relevant municipal government.	

(Continued)

	Developing publicity and exchange platforms	*Supporting the formation of platform and application interaction system*
Anhui		Support platform-based enterprises in the digital economy. Attract independent application developers by making platform functions and data available to them, and also providing the necessary environment and tools. This would result in a positive and interactive environment of development and utilization. A total of 10 million yuan in prize money and subsidies would be provided every year to a selected number of Anhui Province companies that have independently developed successful industrial apps.
Hunan	Organize influential international or national conferences or professional exchanges on Internet and Big Data. A one-off subsidy of RMB 500,000–2 million will be given depending on the scale and importance of the conference or event.	
Tianjin		
Fujian	Organize provincial digital economy entrepreneurship and innovation competitions targeted at third-party organizations or well-known enterprises in the industry, with up to RMB 5 million in prize money for each competition.	
Guangxi		
Guizhou	Since 2015, the annual Big Data Expo has been held for four consecutive years. In 2017, the event was officially upgraded to a national-level exhibition. As the world's first Big Data-themed expo, the Big Data Expo provides its participants with insights into global Big Data development. It is also the most important global platform for the exchange of Big Data findings and ideas.	

8.3.3 Comparison and analysis of provinces, autonomous regions, and municipalities that focus on developing digital ecosystems

Table 8-13   Comparison and analysis of provinces, autonomous regions, and municipalities that focus on developing digital ecosystems

	Supporting innovative public service platforms	*Supporting the development of cloud services and other platforms*
Anhui		Encourage companies to make breakthroughs in key technologies such as data integration, platform management, development tools, microservice frameworks, modeling, and analysis. The building of Industrial Internet (cloud) platforms is also encouraged. A number of enterprise-level Industrial Internet (cloud) platforms will be selected each year and awarded a bonus of RMB 500,000 each. Similarly, a number of Industrial Internet (cloud) public platforms will be selected each year and awarded a bonus of RMB 1 million each. Establish a dynamically managed Industrial Internet (cloud) service resource catalogue. Recognize and commend the efforts of outstanding service providers.
Hunan	Encourage industrial parks, enterprises, and social organizations to build public resource platforms such as application testing platforms, cloud services platforms, data centers, and industry public technical services platforms, and subsequently continue to improve platform support functions. The provincial authorities will provide subsidies not exceeding 20% of platform construction costs, capped at RMB 10 million. This is done to make the public service system more professional, networked, and integrated.	

(Continued)

	Supporting innovative public service platforms	Supporting the development of cloud services and other platforms
Tianjin		
Fujian	An investment subsidy of no more than RMB 5 million will be given to enterprises and institutions (including universities and scientific research institutions) for investments in digital economy innovation platforms and key industries' public platforms.	
Guangxi		The autonomous region supports industry leaders as they invest in the building of public service cloud platforms and shared economy platforms. Following verification, these projects will be subsidized using the relevant service industry special funds. The amount of subsidy is capped at 10% of the actual outlay on the project, and the actual subsidy for a single project shall not exceed RMB 15 million.
Guizhou	Promote the integration of Big Data industry elements, support and encourage enterprises to develop Big Data industry public R&D technology service platforms. For investments of more than RMB 10 million in specialized public R&D technology service platforms, a one-time incentive worth 10% of the investment amount, capped at RMB 10 million, will be granted after verification by the relevant municipal government.	

8.3.4 Comparison and analysis of provinces, autonomous regions, and municipalities that focus on attracting strong companies to cultivate market entities

Table 8-14   Comparison and analysis of provinces, autonomous regions, and municipalities that focus on attracting strong companies to cultivate market entities

Attracting leading companies	
Hunan	
Tianjin	Following verification, Big Data and cybersecurity companies that are leaders in the Chinese market, in terms of overall capability or market share, will receive awards up to RMB 5 million. Following verification, promising Big Data and cybersecurity start-ups will be awarded up to RMB 3 million.
Shanghai	Encourage leading AI companies to establish their headquarters in Shanghai, and encourage companies or organizations that are capable of doing so to set up innovation platforms and incubators. Encourage AI companies to transform their overseas innovation outcomes in Shanghai. Such innovation outcomes would be given the same level of support as if they were obtained in China.
Anhui	1. For electronics, software, and Internet companies among China's Top 100 which build their headquarters (including R&D and regional headquarters) here, a one-time bonus of RMB 2 million each will be provided. 2. Electronics, software, and Internet companies listed among China's Top 100 for the first time will be given a one-time bonus of RMB 1 million each. 3. Companies that are included in the province's list of key electronics, IT, or software companies for the first time will be given a one-time bonus of RMB 500,000 each.
Fujian	Leading digital economy companies which set up independent legal entities (including regional headquarters, industry headquarters, and R&D centers), and with registered capital of RMB 100 million and above, will be given a one-time moving-in incentive of RMB 2 million.
Guizhou	1. Depending on the amount of taxes they pay, jobs they create, and impact on industry standards, Big Data and digital economy companies that shift their headquarters to Guizhou—or establish a regional headquarters there—will be given a one-time moving-in grant of no more than RMB 5 million by the local government. 2. Fortune Global 500, Top 100 Chinese electronics companies, or key companies producing software or integrated circuit designs that are part of national plans will receive support. Projects that invest more than RMB 500 million in Guizhou to set up R&D and production bases will have part of the income from the transfer of rights to use state-owned land go to the local government to be used for financial support of such projects.

(Continued)

	Supporting local companies to grow bigger and stronger
Hunan	1. Reward profit-making software and Internet companies that are listed among China's Top 100. Those that make it to the top 20 will be given a one-time reward of RMB 3 million, those placed between 21–50 will be given a one-time reward of RMB 2 million, and the rest will be given a one-time reward of RMB 1 million. 2. Profitable companies whose mobile Internet or Big Data business income exceeds RMB 100 million, 500 million, and 1 billion for the first time will receive a one-off reward of RMB 500,000, 1 million, and 2 million respectively. The rewards do not affect the company's eligibility to apply for government projects. 3. For small, medium, and micro enterprises with operating revenue greater than RMB 3 million in the previous year and an annual growth rate greater than 50% will be given project funding subsidies between RMB 300,000–1.5 million depending on the project's investment amount, scale, growth rate, economic contribution, and employment. 4. For companies that have obtained investments from angel investors and venture capitalists, more support will be provided depending on the amount of investment obtained.
Tianjin	
Shanghai	
Anhui	For digital technology companies in the province, when operating revenue reaches RMB 100 million and 1 billion for the first time, they will be given a one-time bonus of RMB 1 million and 5 million, respectively. When a company has been included in the national list of unicorns, the local government will be encouraged to provide the company with greater support.
Fujian	Internet companies with annual operating revenue exceeding RMB 40 million and 100 million for the first time will be given a one-off reward of RMB 500,000 and 1 million, respectively. For selected outstanding innovative products in key areas of the digital economy, a one-time award of no more than RMB 2 million will be given based on performance.
Guizhou	1. Allow newly established micro enterprises in Big Data and related industries, if they meet the criteria, to enjoy government support under the "Three RMB 150,000" policy designated for companies in key industries. 2. For Big Data enterprises that have invested RMB 10 million or more, within three years from the first day of operation, all taxes paid by the enterprise to entities below the provincial level will be refunded in full to the enterprise by the local government to support its development. If the enterprise has been operating for more than three years but less than five years, half the taxes will be returned. 3. Recognized leading Big Data companies can receive greater support through differentiated treatment on a case-by-case basis.

8.3.5 Comparison and analysis of provinces, autonomous regions, and municipalities regarding talent incentives and the establishment of academic disciplines

Table 8-15 Comparison and analysis of provinces, autonomous regions, and municipalities regarding talent incentives and the establishment of academic disciplines

	Offering greater accolades for major contributions	*Encouraging the establishment of digital economy majors*	*Providing greater support for technological innovation and entrepreneurship*
Guangxi		For newly approved doctoral, master's, undergraduate, and vocational programs related to Big Data, one-off rewards of RMB 2 million, 1.5 million, 1 million, and 500,000 respectively will be awarded through the autonomous region's education development special fund.	
Hunan		Encourage provincial colleges and universities to cooperate with the relevant units to jointly set up Internet colleges. Provide colleges and universities with subsidies of up to RMB 1 million for establishing mobile internet- and Big Data-related majors.	For teams that generate significant economic benefits through technological research and entrepreneurship in mobile Internet, Big Data, IoT, AI and blockchain technology, five to ten such outstanding teams would be rewarded annually for their innovation with a one-off subsidy of RMB 500,000 to 1 million.

(Continued)

210

	Offering greater accolades for major contributions	Encouraging the establishment of digital economy majors	Providing greater support for technological innovation and entrepreneurship
Anhui	Every year, the top 10 digital economy companies are selected, and each is awarded a one-time bonus of RMB 1 million. The ten digital economy leaders are also recognized and a one-time bonus of RMB 500,000 given to their teams.		
Guizhou			

	Supporting digital economy companies and organizations in training technical talents		
Guangxi	1. Employees of digital economy companies who have bought unemployment insurance in accordance with the law, have paid premiums for at least 36 months, and who have obtained the elementary (Level 5), intermediate (Level 4) or advanced (Level 3) vocational qualification certificate or vocational skills certificate after January 1, 2017, can apply for a one-time skills upgrading subsidy of RMB 1,000, 1,500, or 2,000 respectively. 2. For occupational skills that are urgently needed in the autonomous region, the skills upgrade subsidy will be 20% more than that for skills that are not urgently required. The unemployment insurance fund will be used for the top up.		
Hunan	For institutions of higher learning, secondary vocational schools, technical schools and other education and training institutions that provide mobile Internet and Big Data courses with a duration greater than six months, if more than 200 students from a course go on to sign employment contracts of more than two years with provincial enterprises after graduating, up to RMB 1 million may be given to the school as compensation after taking into account the training costs and the actual number of graduates who signed employment contracts.		
Anhui			

(Continued)

	Supporting digital economy companies and organizations in training technical talents
Guizhou	1. Encourage companies to cooperate with renowned universities and institutes at home and abroad, explore diversified joint training models, and focus on training talents in areas facing talent shortages, such as networking technology, Big Data, AI, and VR. University and research institute personnel can be given leave of absence of up to three years for the purpose of focusing on start-up development. Actively recruit high-level digital economy talents into the provincial leadership and innovation program and prioritize recommending them for selection into the nation's Thousand Talents Program.
	2. Encourage qualified vocational colleges, social training institutions, and digital economy enterprises to carry out online entrepreneurship training. Provide training subsidies in accordance with relevant regulations to workers participating in such trainings. Provide subsidies for employment skills training and highly-skilled personnel training for digital economy-related occupations. Those who participate in vocational training and vocational skills certification, as well as digital economy companies that organize training for their employees, can enjoy training and skills certification subsidies as stipulated.

8.3.6 Comparison and analysis of provinces, autonomous regions, and municipalities that focus on providing more factor resources

Table 8-16 Comparison and analysis of provinces, autonomous regions, and municipalities that focus on providing more factor resources

	Implementing preferential tax policies
Guangxi	
Hunan	
Tianjin	
Anhui	Strictly implement policies such as the accelerated depreciation of fixed assets, the deduction of corporate R&D expenses, income tax incentives for software and integrated circuit companies, and tax incentives for small and micro enterprises. Qualified high-tech enterprises will be taxed at a reduced corporate income tax rate of 15%. Implement the relevant income tax policies for equity incentives and those obtaining equity through their technical expertise.
Fujian	

(Continued)

	Implementing preferential tax policies
Guizhou	1. For qualifying legal person partners of venture capital enterprises and limited partnership venture capital enterprises engaged in start-up investment encouraged by the state, taxable income can be deducted by a certain percentage of the investment amount. 2. Prioritize support for qualified digital economy enterprises to be recognized as high-tech enterprises, so they can enjoy a preferential corporate income tax rate of 15%. 3. New R&D instruments and equipment purchased by the digital economy enterprises, with a unit value that does not exceed RMB 1 million, are entitled to lump sum deduction before tax. If the unit value exceeds RMB 1 million, the depreciation period can be shortened or accelerated depreciation opted for. 4. Preferential tax policies (corporate income tax, value-added tax, etc.) are available for small-scale digital economy start-ups with broad development prospects that are conducive to entrepreneurship and innovation, in accordance with the relevant national tax incentive policies. 5. R&D expenses incurred in the development of new technologies, products, and processes by digital economy enterprises can be deducted when calculating taxable income.
	Increasing funding support
Guangxi	
Hunan	Regulate the operation of the provincial mobile Internet investment fund and actively attract social capital to participate in the fund. Based on the amount invested by the provincial government, any investment income due to the government in excess of the benchmark can be transferred to social capital. For venture capital investing in corporate projects, a one-time subsidy of not more than 20% of the venture capital investment can be given within three years after funds are in place, capped at RMB 2 million.
Tianjin	
Anhui	
Fujian	Encourage financial institutions, industrial capital, and other social capital to establish market-oriented industrial investment funds and venture capital funds in digital economy sectors, such as the IoT, Big Data, AI, and satellite applications. Such funds will invest in unlisted digital economy companies in Fujian in exchange for company shares. For funds that invest RMB 50 million or more annually, a reward equivalent to a portion of the total investment made by the fund that year will be given, capped at RMB 3 million a year.

(Continued)

	Increasing funding support
Guizhou	Hasten the concentration of social capital in the digital economy. Establish a portfolio of digital economy development projects focusing on cutting-edge technical support, digital infrastructure, intelligent transformation and upgrading, etc. Release and promote digital economy engineering projects in a timely manner. Step up the promotion of such projects to business associations, big companies, and conglomerates in Guizhou so that social capital investment in quality digital economy projects is enhanced. Encourage angel investors, venture capitalists, start-up investors, and private equity investors to support the development of digital economy start-ups and companies with good growth potential.
	Increasing credit support
Guangxi	
Hunan	
Tianjin	
Anhui	Encourage financial institutions in the banking industry to optimize the credit approval process and appropriately increase the risk tolerance for loan applications by digital technology companies. To expand the scale of credit loans, such financial institutions can also look into accepting intellectual property, trademarks, patents, equity, and accounts receivable as collateral. Innovate in "tax-based financing" to make loans more readily available to small-and medium-sized enterprises. Establish resource reserves for provincial digital economy companies to go public. The provincial government shall encourage such companies to list in capital markets by rewarding them and supporting companies that qualify for bond issuance. Under the same conditions, state-owned and state-controlled financing guarantee companies will prioritize digital economy enterprises, at rates no higher than 1.2%. Subsidize premiums for technology insurance purchased by high-tech digital economy enterprises.
Fujian	Provide preferential loans for major projects. Provide preferential loans for new investments in infrastructure and major project investments, such as digital economy industrial bases, key industrial parks, innovation platforms, etc. The discount for a single project shall not exceed 50% of the benchmark loan interest rate for the same period issued by the People's Bank of China. The discount shall also be capped at RMB 10 million a year, and provided no more than three years in a row.

(Continued)

	Increasing credit support
Guizhou	Encourage financial institutions to explore accepting intellectual property as collateral for loans. Support foreign venture capital and equity investment organizations to actively explore new management models for investment projects. Groom qualified digital economy companies for public listings. Encourage small- and medium-sized digital economy companies to list on the National Equities Exchange and Quotation. Support qualifying digital economy companies to diversify their financing channels by issuing corporate bonds and non-financial corporate debt financing instruments. Encourage county, city, and district governments, industrial authorities, and industrial park management to provide innovative companies in the digital economy with preferential loans, subsidies, and other financial services.
	Prioritize land for construction
Guangxi	1. With income from the transfer of state-owned land use rights for digital economy industrial base investments greater than RMB 500 million, after withdrawals for various special funds are deducted a portion of the surplus will be retained by the city or county. This can be used to support the construction of the digital economy industrial base per government policy. 2. For companies registered in the Advanced Business Park, rentals for standard factory buildings and office buildings which the local government has a stake in will be subsidized by the local government. If the rental area is smaller than 300 square meters, the rent will be waived; if the rental area is between 300 and 1,000 square meters, the rent will be halved for three years.
Hunan	
Tianjin	For Big Data and cybersecurity companies that move into standard factories or office buildings which the government has invested in, the local government will subsidize rental for three years. If the rental area is smaller than 300 square meters, the rent will be waived; if the rental area is between 300 and 1,000 square meters, the rent will be halved for three years.
Anhui	For projects involving next-generation information networks (except communications facilities), new IT services, e-commerce, etc., land can be used for commercial purposes. On the premise of not changing land usage and planning conditions, the development of Internet resources and the use of real estate stock and land resources to develop new industrial formats, innovative business models, and online/offline integrated businesses can continue to be implemented using transition policies. At the end of the transition period, the land use procedures can be handled separately depending on the business development format and detailed planning control.

(Continued)

Prioritize land for construction	
Fujian	
Guizhou	1. Increase land use security. Build up land reserves first before increasing developments to ensure adequate land supply for the new digital economy industries and formats. For areas with the rapid development of new industries and industrial formats, intensive land use, and high demand, the annual allocation of land for construction can be appropriately increased. For digital economy industrial projects that conform to overall land use and urban-rural plans, land supply will be prioritized. For land designated for digital economy enterprises, under the premise of conforming to the industry direction and clarifying the type of industrial land, bidding can be carried out for land transfer to improve the efficiency of land resource development.
	2. Reduce land costs. For new digital economy projects included in the provincial list of key projects, payment for obtaining state-owned land use rights can be carried out in installments, with 50% of the transfer price paid within one month after signing the land transfer contract and the balance paid within a year. For land-intensive digital economy key projects that are included in the provincial digital economy industry plan, the base price for land transfer can be set at not less than 70% of the minimum for equivalent industrial land parcels in the area, provided it is not lower than the sum of the acquisition cost, initial development cost, and relevant obligatory fees. For digital economy companies that have just moved in, if their annual tax (excluding land use tax) is more than RMB 30,000 per *mu* (around 920 square yards), they will be rewarded by the local government in the five years beginning from their second year of operation. For industrial land used by existing digital economy enterprises, the land price will not be increased if the land utilization rate is increased, so long as it does not compromise government plans and change land use. Encourage the implementation of long-term leasing, lease first buy later, or other combinations of leasing and buying in supplying industrial land. Speed up processing work for industrial park land use. Employees in digital economy industrial clusters and digital economy enterprises who satisfy the relevant criteria can be covered under the local housing guarantee policies.

(Continued)

	Provide greater power supply support
Guangxi	For digital economy industrial parks that have been included in the Guangxi Digital Economy Development Plan (2018–2025), they will also benefit from the power consumption policies available to industrial parks and modern service industry clusters at the autonomous region level and above. Companies located in these industrial parks will be included in the power market. For Big Data center users who are unable to participate in market-based electricity trading and whose unit electricity price is above RMB 0.349 per kWh, a financial subsidy up to RMB 0.20 per kWh will be given (unit electricity price should not be lower than RMB 0.349 per kWh after the subsidy), for three consecutive years, capped at RMB 5 million per user. This will greatly reduce the electricity cost for Big Data centers.
Hunan	Speed up the construction and optimize the distribution of new infrastructure such as cloud computing and Big Data platforms. Data centers with transformer capacities of 315 KVA and above shall be allowed to pay heavy industries electrical tariffs and given priority to purchase electricity directly.
Tianjin	
Anhui	Implement two-part electrical tariffs for eligible cloud computing, supercomputing, data, and disaster management centers. Support communication companies, broadcasting and television companies, and relevant IT companies in transacting directly with power generation companies.
Fujian	
Guizhou	Data centers with transformer capacities of 315 KVA and above shall be allowed to pay heavy industries electrical tariffs and given priority to purchase electricity directly. Encourage Big Data centers to be equipped with their own power plants and reduce their costs by doing so through financial subsidies and incentives.

8.4 Conclusion

The digital economy is an important opportunity for countries to embark on sustainable development. As the fastest growing sector in the global economy, the new economy has become a leading force driving the development of emerging industries, transforming traditional industries, and promoting employment and economic growth. It is directly related to the future direction and state of the global economy.

The digital economy is more than just a new variable for improving the quality and efficiency of the Chinese economy. It is also a vast new ocean for the country's economic transformation and growth. China's government, enterprises, and society should actively carry out digital transformation to promote the healthy development of the digital economy. All parties must strive to create favorable conditions for the development of the digital economy and actively tackle the various problems that may arise, so that technological development truly benefits the masses.

In the process of digital technology empowering conventional industries, industries that are light on operations tend to fully digitalize first, while those that are heavy on operations struggle to transform effectively. The online management of physical operations is complicated and inefficient, the real-time changes of offline information are not reflected online in time, online and offline information are disconnected, and business integration is incomplete. These are problems that prevent the deep integration of the digital economy with traditional industries. How to overcome these, in order to maximize value, has become the primary challenge of the moment in helping traditional industries undergo a complete makeover.

In the future, digital technology must be thoroughly refined to fully digitalize offline products and operations for online management and deployment. Only after the digitalization of physical industries is sufficiently in-depth can open offline management be achieved. The openness of online information provides consumers with an intuitive understanding of product information using data. It also allows online platforms to effectively adjust their offline operations based on consumer feedback. In the future, digital enterprises will use Internet technology to visualize their operational processes and manage product traceability.

With the guidance and security provided by more "down-to-earth" policies, it is likely that the Chinese digital economy will develop in a rapid and healthy fashion. This will pave the way for digital twin technology to become more sophisticated and mature, thus benefiting the country and its people.

AFTERWORD

This is an era of rapid technological development, and for many people, some cutting-edge technologies may seem unfamiliar. However, these cutting-edge technologies are closely related to every individual in the age of technology, and when these technologies make breakthroughs, they may trigger business transformations overnight. Especially for the booming metaverse today, constructing the metaverse would only be possible with the support of digital twin technology. Therefore, from the essence of the metaverse, the so-called metaverse is a digital twin of Earth. It's just that when discussing the term "digital twin of Earth," it feels more technical to the general public. But when packaged as the metaverse, from the perspective of capital speculation, it becomes more propagative and sensational.

The same applies to the artificial intelligence revolution triggered by ChatGPT. When artificial intelligence is involved in our urban governance, it can improve efficiency and make urban governance more scientific and precise. The key lies in constructing a digital twin city to achieve such a vision. Artificial intelligence is just a management tool, while the digital twin city is the underlying core of a smart city.

The essence of China's national initiative of "Digital China" lies in the construction of a digital twin China. This includes digitization in healthcare, education, management, manufacturing, commerce, and research. If we simplify the concept, the so-called "Digital China" is essentially the digitization of tangible physical entities of the entire country, including its people. And the key technology for this digitization is digital twins, which essentially constructs a digital twin nation.

The construction of a digital twin nation extends downwards to the construction of digital cities and upwards to the construction of a digital Earth. A new era of virtual and real-world interconnectedness and interaction is being established based on digital twin technology and linking cutting-edge technologies, such as quantum computing,

DNA storage, satellite communication, artificial intelligence, brain-machine interfaces, and virtual reality. We currently call this new era the metaverse, but it can be foreseen that when the true era of the metaverse arrives, it will no longer be called the metaverse. We, as humans, will redefine that era based on its culture, civilization, and forward-thinking technology.

The future is propelling humanity into the digital age at a pace beyond our imagination, and digital twins are the indispensable underlying technology for the present and future, for Digital China and digital Earth.

NOTES

1. Datong Liu et al., "Digital Twin Technology—Overview and Outlook," *Chinese Journal of Scientific Instrument*, no. 11 (2018).
2. Ibid.
3. Deloitte, *Industry 4.0 and Digital Twin to Boost Manufacturing*, 2018.
4. Ibid.
5. "How to Create Digital Twins," https://www2.deloitte.com/cn/zh/pages/consumerindustrial-products/articles/industry-4-0-and-the-digital-twin.html.
6. Deloitte, *Industry 4.0 and Digital Twin to Boost Manufacturing*, 2018.
7. Cunbo Zhuang et al., "The Connotation, Architecture, and Development Trend of Product Digital Twins," *Computer Integrated Manufacturing Systems Journal*, no. 23 (2017): 4.
8. "How to Understand and Apply the Digital Twin Concept," http://sh.qihoo.com/pc/9cf5c809c89b80f5c?cota=3& refer_scene=so_1&sign=360_e39369d1.
9. Cunbo Zhuang et al., "The Connotation, Architecture, and Development Trend of Product Digital Twins," *Computer Integrated Manufacturing Systems Journal*, no. 23 (2017): 4.
10. "100 Terms of Industry 4.0," September 1, 2020, http://www.hysim.cc/view.php?id=81.
11. "Novel Industry 4.0 Concept: Digital Twin—Digitization of Manufacturing Processes Boosts the Industry," September 2, 2020, https://www.iyiou.com/intelligence/insight65822.html.
12. "The Application and Significance of Digital Twin," http://www.clii.com.cn/lhrh/hyxx/201810/t20181008_3924192.html.
13. Cunbo Zhuang et al., "The Connotation, Architecture, and Development Trend of Product Digital Twins," *Computer Integrated Manufacturing Systems Journal*, no. 23 (2017): 4.
14. "The Main Roles and Application of Digital Twin," http://articles.e-works.net.cn/plmoverview/Article139176_1.html.
15. Cunbo Zhuang et al., "The Connotation, Architecture, and Development Trend of Product Digital Twins," *Computer Integrated Manufacturing Systems Journal*, no. 23 (2017): 4.
16. Ibid.
17. "Understanding Digital Twin through Simulation," September 14, 2020, http://www.sohu.com/a/195717460_488176.
18. "The 8 Interpretations of Digital Twin," September 14, 2020, https://www.cnblogs.com/aabbcc/p/10000117.html.
19. Cunbo Zhuang et al., "The Connotation, Architecture and Development Trend of Product Digital Twin," *Computer Integrated Manufacturing Systems Journal*, no. 23 (2017): 4.
20. Source from: China Academy of Information and Communications Technology.

21. Cai Chen, "Digital Twin City Service Forms and Characteristics," *CAICT informatization research.*

22. Gao Yanli, "Promoting the Building of Smart Cities with Digital Twin City," *CAICT informatization research.*

23. "What Is Digital Twin Technology and What Value Does It Offer?" http://field.10jqka.com.cn/20190313/c610219150.shtml.

24. "The Rise of the Digital Twin Concept, and Its Exploration and Application in Various Fields," https://tech.china.com/article/20190312/kejiyuan012 9252569.html.

25. "Computer Integrated Manufacturing Systems" Editorial Board, "Digital Twin Series Report 10—Complex Product Assembly Process Driven by Digital Twin."

26. "Twin Win for Oil and Gas Production," 14 September 2020, https://www.bp.com/en/global/corporate/news-and-insights/reimagining-energy/apex-digital-system.html.

27. "Digital Twin: Future Comprehensive Budgeting Systems," https://www.xuanruanjian.com/art/146214.phtm.

28. Xiong Ming et al., "Building and Using an In-Service Oil and Gas Pipeline Digital Twin for the First Time in China," *Oil and Gas Storage and Transportation,* 2019.

29. Tao Fei et al., "The Five-Dimensional Digital Twin Model and 10 Major Applications," *Computer Integrated Manufacturing Systems,* no. 25 (2019): 1.

30. Ibid.

31. Ibid.

32. Ibid.

REFERENCES

1. "A New Era—The Digital Twin City." *Information China.*
2. Cai Chen. "Digital Twin City Service Forms and Characteristics." *CAICT informatization research.*
3. Cunbo Zhuang et al. "The Connotation, Architecture, and Development Trend of Product Digital Twins."
4. Deloitte. *Industry 4.0 and Digital Twin to Boost Manufacturing.* 2018.
5. *Computer Integrated Manufacturing Systems Journal.* 2017.
6. "Digital Twin—100 Industry 4.0 Terms." http://www.hysim.cc/view. php?id=81.
7. "Digital Twin: Future Comprehensive Budgeting Systems." https://www.xuanruanjian.com /art/146214.phtm.
8. "Digital Twin in IoT Applications—A Comprehensive IoT Digital Twin Solution." https:// blog.csdn.net/steelren/article/details/79198165.
9. "Digital Twin Series Report 10—Complex Product Assembly Process Driven by Digital Twin." *Computer Integrated Manufacturing Systems.*
10. "Understanding Digital Twin through Simulation." http://www.sohu.com/a/ 195717460_488176.
11. "The 8 Interpretations of Digital Twin." https://www.cnblogs.com/aabbcc/p/10000117.html.
12. Gartner. "Digital Twins Going Mainstream, 75% of Organizations Implementing IoT Already Use Digital Twins or Plan to Within 5 Years." http://sh.qihoo.com/ pc/9b8c49be3ce053038?cota=3&refer_scene=so_1&sign=360_e39369d1.
13. "How to Understand and Apply the Digital Twin Concept." http://sh.qihoo.com/ pc/9cf5c809c89b80f5c?cota=3& refer_scene=so_1&sign=360_e39369d1.
14. Liu Datong et al. "Digital Twin Technology—Overview and Outlook." *Chinese Journal of Scientific Instrument,* no. 11 (2018).
15. Neucloud. "The Application and Significance of Digital Twin." http://www.clii.com.cn/lhrh /hyxx/201810/t20181008_3924192.html.
16. "Replicating a City in Virtual Space! Using Digital Twin Cities to Drive the Building of Smart Cities." http://news.rfidworld.com.cn/2019_02/32c97e1975b284b7.html.
17. Tao Fei et al. "The Five-Dimensional Digital Twin Model and 10 Major Applications." *Computer Integrated Manufacturing Systems,* no. 25 (2019).

18. "The Rise of the Digital Twin Concept, and Its Exploration and Application in Various Fields." https://tech.china.com/article/20190312/kejiyuan012 9252569.html.

19. "Using Digital Twin Technology to Boost Production." https://mp.weixin.qq.com/s? biz= MzU1MTkwNDAwOA%3 D%3D&idx=2&mid=2247491107&sn=b5556beff5dee5f57c2dbe 39bca7c6f1.

20. "What Is Digital Twin Technology and What Value Does It Offer?" http://field.10jqka.com. cn/20190313/c610219150.shtml.

21. Xiong Ming et al. "Building and Using an In-Service Oil and Gas Pipeline Digital Twin for the First Time in China." *Oil and Gas Storage and Transportation*, no. 38 (2019).

22. Yanli Gao. "Promoting the Building of Smart Cities with Digital Twin City." *CAICT Informatization Research*.

INDEX

A

Accurate mapping, 92, 148
aerial photogrammetry, 127, 130, 133, 135
aircraft digital, 11
aircraft digital twin, 11, 65
Air Force Research Laboratory (AFRL), 5, 10,
    11–13, 85, 108–10
Ansys, 17, 33, 76, 81–82, 147
APEX, 123–4
Apollo program, 7, 9, 10, 12
AR technology, 87
Asset Administration Shell (AAS), 31–32
Assets Performance Management (APM), 12

B

Big Data technology, 19, 113
Biological human body, 170–1
BOM, 67, 70–71, 75
Building Information Modeling (BIM), 13, 96,
    136

C

Centerline detection, 133
Chief Information Officer (CIO), 27, 40
city service records, 175
cloud, viii, 5, 17, 22, 24, 26, 32–34, 42–43,
    50–52, 54, 80–81, 83, 86, 89–90, 92, 97–
    99, 121, 126, 128–32, 134–6, 141, 168,
    176, 195, 197–9, 200–204, 214

complex electromechanical equipment, 151,
    164
computer-aided design, 27
conceptual architecture, 52–53, 55
Cyber-Physical Systems, 30, 115, 119, 121, 141

D

Data verification and alignment, 127–31
digital data, 4, 75, 86, 144–5, 190
digital economic growth, 183
digital economy, 182–3, 185, 187–9, 191–7,
    199, 201–2, 204–15
digital images, 7, 19, 39
digital means, 2, 12, 18, 21–22, 72, 75
digital model design, 69
digital products, 61–62
digital prototype, 61–62
digital threads, 5, 6, 8
digital thread technology, 86–87
digital twin city, v, viii, 88, 89, 90, 92, 93, 94,
    95, 96, 97, 99, 175, 217
digital twin data, 141, 146, 155, 156, 157, 158,
    159, 160, 163, 165, 167, 170, 171, 173
Digital Twin Enterprise (DTE), 39
Digital Twin Organization (DTO), 39
digital twin(s), v, viii, ix, 1–7, 9–15, 17–24,
    26–34, 36–37, 39–40, 42–45, 47–66, 69,
    71–75, 77, 79–87, 90–97, 99–101, 103,
    106–9, 111, 113–7, 119–23, 125–7, 135,

137–146, 148–53, 155–7, 159, 161–2, 164, 166, 168–9, 171–82, 215, 217–8
digital twin technology, 88
digital twin vehicle, 159
distributed cloud server storage technology, 42
distributed sensing technology, 42

E
Encompassing the entire lifecycle, 85
Enterprise Performance Management (EPM), 125–6
Enterprise Resource Planning (ERP), 53–54, 125–7, 137
equipment integrity management, 173

F
failure prediction and integrity management, 156
fault prediction and integrity management, 157
five-dimensional digital twin model, ix, 145–6, 152, 155, 157, 162, 164, 166–7, 171, 174
full lifecycle data management, 42
full three-dimensional model, 7

G
General Electric (GE), 12–13, 17, 33, 64, 81–82, 109

H
high-performance computers, 108
high-performance computing, 51–52, 77
human body digital twin, 171–2

I
Industrial Internet, 26, 28, 34, 60, 77, 86, 115, 140, 143, 197, 200, 203
Industry 4.0, v, viii, 4, 22, 31–32, 60, 79, 115
intelligent assembly, 115, 119, 122
Intelligent assembly technology, 117
intelligent manufacturing, 4, 108, 113, 115, 141, 143, 168, 172, 185, 192, 195
Interaction between virtual and real, 92

L
lifecycle data management, 41, 47, 50, 74
lightweight model technology, 76–77

M
Measuring reference points, 132
model-based definition (MBD), 75–76, 87, 114–5, 118
Modeling, 4, 5, 12, 20, 37, 40–49, 51, 62–63, 67–68, 71, 76, 85, 87, 91–92, 118–20, 122, 125, 127, 134, 144, 147–8, 156, 162, 166, 169, 172, 174, 185, 200, 203
Multidimensional data warehouse software and applications, 125
multidomain modeling, 47

O
Oblique photogrammetry of stations, 135
Oracle, 83, 89

P
payload, 103, 152
personal health management, 151, 169, 171, 180
physical city, 88, 90–92, 99, 174–6
physical entities, 4, 13, 19, 21, 23, 26, 29–32, 34, 37, 57, 120, 140, 143–4, 146, 177, 217
pipeline data asset library, 135–6
pipeline midline detection, 127
process design, 5, 6, 52–53, 67, 70–71, 75–76, 86–87, 114–6, 118, 120, 122, 156
product digital twin(s), 7–8, 61–62, 64–70, 74–79, 84–87
product full lifecycle, 17
product lifecycle, 4, 7, 9, 11–12, 15–19, 22, 52, 61–62, 66–70, 74–75, 83, 86, 115
Product Lifecycle Management (PLM), viii, 9, 19, 23, 26, 28, 67, 69–70, 82, 108, 115
product's digital twin(s), 7
prognostics and health management (PHM), 154–5, 164, 166
PTC, 82–83

R

reduced order model (ROM), 109
remote monitoring, 73, 101, 151, 180

S

satellite network digital twin, 153
satellite network nodes, 153
satellite/space communication networks,
    151–4
sensor technology, 42, 49, 79
Siemens, viii, 1, 33, 38–39, 80–81
simulation technology, 45, 68, 82, 87
smart city, 89–91, 95–97, 174–6, 217
smart homes, 101, 151, 176–7
smart logistics, 103, 151, 177–9, 190
smart services, 36, 96, 140, 142–3, 175
space information network digital twin, 153
space information network(s), 152–4
station data asset library, 136
stereoscopic warehouse, 151, 166–8, 178

T

3D assembly process design, 115–22
3D laser scanner, 134
3D laser scanning, 127, 131, 134–5, 161
3D model(s), 32, 63, 70–71, 76, 78, 85, 114–5,

117–8, 120, 128–9, 131, 134–6, 147, 161
3D model of the underground pipe network,
    161
3D terrain map construction, 135
3D terrain model, 132–3
tracing and simulation technologies, 79

U

universal industrial interconnection, 140, 143,
    146

V

virtual assembly, 10, 19, 118–9, 143, 148
virtual assembly technology, 115, 118–9
virtual city, 40, 88, 91, 174–5
virtual digital, 9, 41, 46
virtual entities, 143–4, 146
virtual human body, 170–2
virtual mapping, 3, 41, 50, 62–63, 164
virtual-real interaction, 143, 164
virtual reality (VR), 2, 12, 17, 19, 20, 22, 23,
    25, 35, 40, 47, 50–51, 58, 64, 79, 87–88,
    93–94, 97, 113, 141, 148, 179–81, 184,
    194–5, 209, 218
virtual sensors, 29

ABOUT THE AUTHOR

Kevin Chen is a renowned science and technology writer and scholar. He was a visiting scholar at Columbia University, a postdoctoral scholar at the University of Cambridge, and an invited course professor at Peking University. He has served as a special commentator and columnist for the *People's Daily*, CCTV, China Business Network, SINA, NetEase, and many other media outlets. He has published monographs in numerous domains, including finance, science and technology, real estate, medical treatments, and industrial design. He currently lives in Hong Kong.